SYNGRESS®

Joe Grand's

"BEST OF" HARDWARE, WIRELESS & GAME CONSOLE HACKING

INCLUDES DVD WITH 20 HACKS IN HIGH-RES COLOR

Joe Grand, Frank Thornton, Albert Yarusso, Lee Barken, Marcus R. Brown,
Job de Haas, Deborah Kaplan, Bobby Kinstle, Tom Owad, and Ryan Russell
Technical Reviewers: Kevin D. Mitnick and Job de Haas

KEY	**SERIAL NUMBER**
001	HJIRTCV764
002	PO9873D5FG
003	829KM8NJH2
004	BZZ2317JMP
005	CVPLQ6WQ23
006	VBP965T5T5
007	HJJJ863WD3E
008	2987GVTWMK
009	629MP5SDJT
010	IMWQ295T6T

PUBLISHED BY
Syngress Publishing, Inc.
800 Hingham Street
Rockland, MA 02370

Joe Grand's Best of Hardware, Wireless, and Game Console Hacking

Printed in Canada.
1 2 3 4 5 6 7 8 9 0
ISBN: 1597491136
Technical Reviewers: Kevin D. Mitnick, *Hardware Hacking*
Job de Haas, *Game Console Hacking*

Distributed by O'Reilly Media, Inc. in the United States and Canada.
For information on rights, translations, and bulk sales, contact Matt Pedersen, Director of Sales and Rights, at Syngress Publishing; email matt@syngress.com or fax to 781-681-3585.

Technical Editor & Contributor

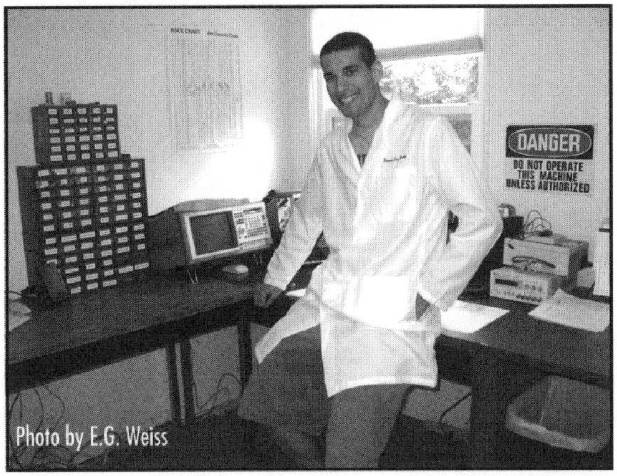

Joe Grand; Grand Idea Studio, Inc. Joe Grand is the President of Grand Idea Studio, a San Diego-based product development and intellectual property licensing firm, where he specializes in the invention and design of consumer electronics, medical devices, video games, and toys. His latest creations include the Stelladaptor Atari 2600 Controller-to-USB Interface and the Emic Text-to-Speech Module.

A recognized figure in computer security, Joe has testified before the United States Senate Governmental Affairs Committee and is a former member of the legendary hacker collective L0pht Heavy Industries. Joe's research on mobile devices and embedded security has been published in various periodicals, including *Circuit Cellar* and the *Digital Investigation Journal.* He is the author of many security-related software tools, including pdd, the first forensic acquisition application for Palm devices. Joe currently has a patent pending on a hardware-based computer memory imaging concept and apparatus (U.S. Patent Serial No. 10/325,506).

Joe has presented his work at numerous academic, industry, and private forums, including the United States Air Force Office of Special Investigations, the Naval Postgraduate School, the IBM Thomas J. Watson Research Center, the Embedded Systems Conference, the Black Hat Briefings, and DEFCON. He has appeared in documentaries and news for television, airplane in-flight programming, and print media outlets. He has also authored *Hardware Hacking: Have Fun While Voiding Your Warranty* (Syngress Publishing, ISBN: 1-932266-83-6), contributed to *Stealing The Network: How to Own A Continent* (Syngress, ISBN: 1-931836-05-1), and is a frequent contributor to other texts. Joe holds a Bachelor of Science degree in Computer Engineering from Boston University.

Joe is the author of "Tools of the Warranty Voiding Trade," "Case Modifications: Building an Atari 2600PC," "Nintendo GBA," and "GP32."

Contributors

Lee Barken (CISSP, CCNA, MCP, CPA) is the co-director of the Strategic Technologies and Research (STAR) Center at San Diego State University. He has worked as an IT consultant and network security specialist for Ernst & Young's Information Technology Risk Management (ITRM) practice and KPMG's Risk and Advisory Services (RAS) practice. Lee is the co-founder of the San Diego Wireless Users Group and writes and speaks on the topic of wireless LAN technology and security. He is the technical editor for *Mobile Business Advisor Magazine*, and the author of *How Secure Is Your Wireless Network? Safeguarding Your Wi-Fi LAN* (ISBN: 0-13-140206-4).

> "Let's be grateful for those who give us happiness; they are the charming gardeners who make our soul bloom." —Marcel Proust

With deepest appreciation for my charming gardeners, a special thank you to my love Stephanie, my mom and dad, Frieda and Israel, my brothers, Derren and Martin, my sister Randi and her husband Scott, my Uncle Harry and my Grandmother Sophie. Thank you for your support and love.

Lee is the author of "Wireless 802.11 Hacks."

Marcus R. Brown is a software engineer at Budcat Creations. His work includes writing low-level drivers and system-level programming such as resource management, file loading, and audio streaming. He is currently working on an unannounced title for the PlayStation 2 and Xbox. Marcus lives in Las Vegas, Nevada.

Marcus is the author of "PlayStation 2."

Christopher Dolberg is a full-time student, and an avid player of console and PC games. When not gaming, he can be found modifying his hardware in an attempt to push it to the very limits of its function. Occasionally he takes time off from both these activities to actually attend classes. He resides in Vermont.

Chris is a contributor to "Xbox."

Frank (Thorn) Thornton runs his own technology-consulting firm, Blackthorn Systems, which specializes in wireless networks. His specialties include wireless network architecture, design, and implementation, as well as network troubleshooting and optimization. An interest in amateur radio has also helped him bridge the gap between computers and wireless networks. Frank's experience with computers goes back to the 1970's when he started programming mainframes. Over the last 30 years, he has used dozens of different operating systems and programming languages. Having learned at a young age which end of the soldering iron was hot, he has even been known to repair hardware on occasion. In addition to his computer and wireless interests, Frank was a law enforcement officer for many years. As a detective and forensics expert he has investigated approximately one hundred homicides and thousands of other crime scenes. Combining both professional interests, he was a member of the workgroup that established ANSI Standard *ANSI/NIST-CSL 1-1993 Data Format for the Interchange of Fingerprint Information*. He has co-authored *WarDriving: Drive, Detect, and Defend: A Guide to Wireless Security* (Syngress Publishing, ISBN: 1-93183-60-3), as well as contributed to *IT Ethics Handbook: Right and Wrong for IT Professionals* (Syngress, ISBN: 1-931836-14-0). He resides in Vermont with his wife.

Frank is the author of "Xbox."

Job de Haas is Managing Director of ITSX BV, a Dutch company located in Amsterdam. ITSX BV provides security testing services in the broadest sense. Job is involved in testing, researching, and breaking security aspects of the latest technologies for corporate clients. In assignments for telecommunication operators and mobile phone manufacturers, Job gained experience with the internal operations of modern phones.

Job holds a master's degree in electrical engineering from Delft Technical University. He previously held positions at the Dutch Aerospace Agency (NLR) as a robotics researcher and at Digicash BV as a developer of cryptographic applications. He lives in Amsterdam, The Netherlands.

Job is the author of "Can You Hear Me Now? Nokia 6210 Mobile Phone Modifications."

Jonathan S. Harbour has been an avid hacker for many years, having started with early systems like the Commodore PET, Apple II, and Tandy 1000. He holds a degree in computer information systems, enjoys writing code in C, C++, and several other languages, and has experience with many platforms, including Windows, Linux, Pocket PC, and Game Boy Advance. Jonathan has written several books on the subject of game programming, and may be contacted via his Web site at www.jharbour.com.

Jonathan is a contributor to "Nintendo GBA."

Deborah Kaplan (PCP) is an independent consultant focusing on revision control systems, system administration tools, release engineering, and open-source software. Deborah has developed enterprise-wide technology infrastructure, integrating telecommunications with heterogeneous Windows and UNIX environments. She specializes in building tools that automate repetitive tasks and monitor systems for performance tuning.

Deborah holds a bachelor's degree from Haverford College and a master's degree from Simmons.

Deborah is the author of "Operating Systems Overview" and "Coding 101."

Bobby Kinstle works in the Reliability Engineering department at Apple Computer, Inc. where he performs destructive simulations of extreme use and abuse of the products. His specialties are performing voltage and frequency margin analysis as well as detailed thermal performance studies. He also performs environmental testing, mechanical shock and vibration, and repetitive stress testing. Bobby also designed and built the lab's test network of over 600-switched Ethernet ports with 4-gigabit fiber optic backbones and NetBoot servers as well as the department data center. When projects are slow Bobby teaches Mac OS X Server training classes within the company.

Bobby is the author of "Terabyte FireWire Hard Drive Case Mod" and a co-author of "Macintosh Hacks."

Tom Owad is the owner and Web master of Applefritter, www.applefritter.com, a community where the artist and the engineer meet. Applefritter provides its members with discussion boards for the exchange of ideas and hosts countless member-contributed hardware hacks and other projects. Tom is pursuing a Bachelor's Degree in Computer Science and International Affairs from Lafayette College, Pennsylvania.

Tom is a co-author of "Macintosh Hacks."

Ryan Russell has worked in the IT field for over 13 years, focusing on information security for the last seven. He was the primary author of *Hack Proofing Your Network, Second Edition* (Syngress Publishing, ISBN 1-928994-70-9) and *Stealing the Network: How to Own the Box*, Syngress Publishing (ISBN: 1-931836-87-6, and is a frequent technical editor for the Hack Proofing series of books. He is also a technical advisor to Syngress Publishing's *Snort 2.0 Intrusion Detection* (ISBN: 1-931836-74-4). Ryan founded the `vuln-dev` mailing list, and moderated it for three years under the alias "Blue Boar." He is a frequent lecturer at security conferences, and can often be found participating in security mailing lists and website discussions. Ryan is the Director of Software Engineering for AnchorIS.com, where he's developing the anti-worm product, Enforcer. One of Ryan's favorite activities is disassembling worms.

Ryan is the author of "Home Theater PCs."

Albert Yarusso is a principle of Austin Systems (www.austinsystems.com), an Austin, Texas-based firm that specializes in web design programming and hosting services. Albert's background consists of a wide range of projects as a software developer, with his most recent experience focused in the game industry. Albert previously worked for Looking Glass Technologies and more recently for Ion Storm Austin, where he helped create the highly acclaimed PC game Deus Ex.

Albert co-founded AtariAge (www.atariage.com) in 2001, a comprehensive website devoted to preserving the history of Atari's rich legacy of video game consoles and computers, which has become one of the busiest destinations on the web for classic gaming fans. In 2003, Albert helped bring the first annual Austin Gaming Expo (www.austingamingexpo.com) to Austin, an extremely successful event that drew over 2,000 visitors in its first year. Albert is also a contributor to *Hardware Hacking: Have Fun While Voiding Your Warranty* (Syngress Publishing, ISBN: 1-932266-83-6).

Albert is the author of "Atari 2600," "Atari 5200 SuperSystem," and "Atari 7800."

Technical Reviewers

Kevin D. Mitnick is a security consultant to corporations worldwide and a cofounder of Defensive Thinking, a Las Vegas-based consulting firm (www.defensivethinking.com). He has testified before the Senate Committee on Governmental Affairs on the need for legislation to ensure the security of the government's information systems. His articles have appeared in major new magazines and trade journals, and he has appeared on Court TV, *Good Morning America*, *60 Minutes*, CNN's *Burden of Proof* and *Headline News*, and has been a keynote speaker at numerous industry events. He has also hosted a weekly radio show on KFI AM 640, Los Angeles. Kevin is also author of the best-selling book, *The Art of Deception: Controlling the Human Element of Security*. Kevin was the Technical Reviewer for *Hardware Hacking*.

Job de Haas is Managing Director of ITSX BV, a Dutch company located in Amsterdam. ITSX BV provides security testing services in the broadest sense. Job is involved in testing, researching, and breaking security aspects of the latest technologies for corporate clients. In assignments for telecommunication operators and mobile phone manufacturers, Job gained experience with internal operations of modern phones.

Job holds a master's degree in electrical engineering from Delft Technical University. He previously held positions at the Dutch Aerospace Agency (NLR) as a robotics researcher and at Digicash BV as a developer of cryptographic applications. He lives in Amsterdam, The Netherlands. Job was the Technical Reviewer for *Game Console Hacking*.

Contents

Introduction 2.0

The way we customize our things says a lot about who we are.

Today, everywhere we look, we are surrounded by a convergence of media – videogames, advertisements, and television. We are told what to believe, how to think, and how to act. We are told what's cool and what's not, what we should buy, what we should wear, and what music we should listen to.

Hardware hacking has never been about what the mainstream media thinks. It's about creativity, education, experimentation, personalization, and just having fun. This book is no different.

Game Console Hacking focuses on modifying our favorite videogame systems to do things they were never intended to do, to add features that we've always wanted but the vendors never gave us, or to create something that has never been done before.

This book is a little bit different than what you might be used to. We cover a wide spectrum of gaming consoles, from the retro and arguably archaic Atari systems, to the teenaged Nintendo NES console, up through the modern consoles like Xbox and PlayStation 2. There's something in here for every type of gamer, whether you like to get your hands dirty with modifying hardware or whether you're an aspiring game developer. Step-by-step hacks are presented with a slew of pictures to hold your hand along the way, as well as resources to let you jump right in to creating your own games for the systems. It's all about education and inspiring you, the reader, to break the mold of what's considered "acceptable." And best of all, you can do so in the comfort of your own home, without breaking any laws.

Long gone are the days where a few guys can make millions on a self-published videogame they designed in Mom's garage. But, the thrill for homebrew game development is still there; and, it has close ties to hardware hacking in that you are giving the system a touch of your personal creativity, doing things the way you want to. It gives us a sense of ownership that a faceless company can't provide.

There is an underbelly to the videogame industry, which nowadays just seems to only sell multi-million dollar productions with gameplay based on franchise licenses and the same, overused 3D game engines. There are thriving development communities for all the systems we cover in this book. There are people who still yearn to develop games just so they can *play* those games. Sharing code samples, socializing with fellow programmers, hacking videogame systems to allow them to run their custom software, designing games for the sheer thrill of the kill. For gamers, by gamers.

There's something to be said for pouring your heart and soul into a creative game design or hardware hack, and I hope this book will entice you to do so. Inspiration and creativity can't be taught or forced. The possibilities are endless.

The way we customize our things says a lot about who we are.

Who are you?

—Joe Grand, author,
hardware hacker, and gamer
July 2004

Introduction 1.0

Hardware hacking. Mods. Tweaks. Though the terminology is new, the concepts are not: A gearhead in the 1950s adding a custom paint job and turbo-charged engine to his Chevy Fleetline, a '70s teen converting his ordinary bedroom into a "disco palace of love," complete with strobe lights and a high-fidelity eight-track system, or a technogeek today customizing his computer case to add fluorescent lighting and slick artwork. Taking an ordinary piece of equipment and turning it into a personal work of art. Building on an existing idea to create something better. These types of self-expression can be found throughout recorded history.

When Syngress approached me to write *Hardware Hacking: Have Fun While Voiding Your Warranty*, our first book on hardware hacking, I knew they had hit the nail on the head. Where else could a geek like me become an artistic genius? Combining technology with creativity and a little bit of skill opened up the doors to a whole new world: hardware hacking.

But why do we do it? The reasons might be different for all of us, but the result is usually the same. We end up with a unique thing that we can call our own—imagined in our minds and crafted through hours, days, or years of effort. *And* doing it on our own terms.

Hardware hacking today has hit the mainstream market like never before. Computer stores sell accessories to customize your desktop PC. Web sites are popping up like unemployed stock brokers to show off the latest hacks. Just about any piece of hardware can serve as a candidate to be hacked. Creativity and determination can get you much farther than most product developers could ever imagine. Hardware hacking is usually an individual effort, like creating a piece of art. However, just like artists, hackers sometimes collaborate and form communities of folks working toward a similar goal.

The use of the term *hacker* is a double-edged sword and often carries a mythical feel. Contrary to the way major media outlets enjoy using the word to describe criminals breaking into computer systems, a hacker can simply be defined as somebody involved in the exploration of technology. And a *hack* in the technology world usually defines a new and novel creation or method of solving a problem, typically in an unorthodox fashion.

The philosophy of most hardware hackers is straightforward:

- Do something with a piece of hardware that has never been done before.
- Create something extraordinary.
- Harm nobody in the process.

Hardware hacking arguably dates back almost 200 years. Charles Babbage created his difference engine in the early 1800s—a mechanical form of hardware hacking. William Crookes discovered the electron in the mid-1800s—possibly the first form of electronics-related hardware hacking. Throughout the development of wireless telegraphy, vacuum tubes, radio, television, and transistors, there have been hardware hackers—Benjamin Franklin, Thomas Edison, and Alexander Graham Bell, to name a few. As the newest computers of the mid-20th century were developed, the ENIAC, UNIVAC, and IBM mainframes, people from those academic institutions fortunate enough to have the hardware came out in droves to experiment. With the development and release of the first microprocessor (Intel 4004) in November 1971, the general public finally got a taste of computing. The potential for hardware hacking has grown tremendously in the past decade as computers and technology have become more intertwined with the mainstream and everyday living.

Hardware hacks can be classified into four different categories, though sometimes a hack falls into more than one:

1. **Personalization and customization** Think "hot rodding for geeks," the most prevalent of hardware hacking. This includes things such as case modifications, custom skins and ring tones, and art projects like creating an aquarium out of a vintage computer.
2. **Adding functionality** Making the system or product do something it wasn't intended to do. This includes things such as converting the iPod to run Linux, implementing a serial port interface on your PlayStation 2, or modifying the Atari 2600 to support stereo sound.
3. **Capacity or performance increase** Enhancing or otherwise upgrading a product. This includes things such as adding memory to your favorite personal digital assistant (PDA), modifying your wireless network card to support an external antenna, or overclocking your PC's motherboard.
4. **Defeating protection and security mechanisms** This includes things such as removing the unique identifier from CueCat barcode scanners, finding Easter eggs and hidden menus in a TiVo or DVD player, or creating a custom cable to unlock the secrets of your cell phone.

Creating your own hardware hacks and product modifications requires at least a basic knowledge of hacking techniques, reverse engineering skills, and a background in electronics and coding. All the information you'll need is in the pages of this book. And if a topic isn't covered in intimate detail, we include references to materials that do. If you just want to do the hack without worrying about the underlying theory behind it, you can do that, too. The step-by-step sections throughout each chapter include pictures and "how to" instructions. The details are in separate sections that you can skip right over and get to the fun part—voiding your warranty!

This book has something for everyone from the beginner hobbyist with little to no electronics or coding experience to the self-proclaimed "gadget geek" and advanced technologist. It is one of the first books to bring hardware hacking to the mainstream. It is meant to be fun and will demystify many of the hacks you have seen and heard about. We, all the contributors to this project, hope you enjoy reading this book and that you find the hacks as exciting and satisfying as we have.

If your friends say "Damn, now *that's* cool," then you know you've done it right.

—Joe Grand, the hardware hacker
formerly known as Kingpin
January 2004

Chapter 1

Tools of the Warranty-Voiding Trade

Topics in this chapter:

- Introduction
- The Essential Tools
- Basic Hardware Hacking
- Advanced Projects and Reverse Engineering
- Where to Obtain the Tools

Introduction

Before you start your hacking projects, you'll need the right arsenal of tools. For some hacks, you might need only a single screwdriver. For others, you could need a workshop complete with power tools and advanced electronic equipment. For the most part, it isn't necessary to have a world-class laboratory or top-of-the-line computer system to conduct most levels of game console hacking. However, it's amazing how much easier things are if you have the right tools for the job.

Besides the physical tools you will need for hardware hacking that we list in this chapter, you'll need a computer system for any adventures into homebrew game development. After deciding on the game console you'll be programming for, you can choose your development system based on the tools that you'll need. Depending on the console you are writing games for, the appropriate development tools might run only on a specific platform (such as Windows, Macintosh, or Linux). Typically, a desktop or laptop PC running Windows 2000/XP with minimum specifications of 1GHz processor, 256MB RAM, 20GB hard drive, and decent graphics card will be sufficient. The more complex and processor-intensive the development tool or emulator, the more powerful your machine needs to be.

The tools and supplies listed in this chapter are merely a baseline of any good hardware hacking cache. We don't list every possible tool in existence, because there is usually more than one solution to any given problem. Think of this section as telling you about the supplies you'll want in your "kitchen," with each hack containing the actual "recipe" you'll cook with. Each hack presented on the DVD provides a list of the specific tools and components you'll need to pull it off.

We include a selection of pictures that show some of the more unique tools of the warranty-voiding trade. These lists will give you an idea of what you'll need to get a good start so you can jump in and get down to hacking.

We have separated the listings into three parts:

- The Essential Tools
- Basic Hardware Hacking
- Advanced Projects and Reverse Engineering

The work area where your activities take place should be a clean, smooth, and well-lit area where you can easily organize and handle parts and/or documentation without losing them. An inexpensive sheet of white poster board makes an excellent construction surface while providing protection for the underlying table or desk.

Warning: Personal Injury

Safety is an important consideration. With many of the tools listed here, improper or careless use can lead to accidents and personal injury. Please take the time to read all necessary instruction manuals and safety documentation before starting your hack. Be sure to wear protective gear at all times, keep your work area free of unnecessary clutter, use a suitable stand for your soldering iron, and avoid tangling the cords of your various tools.

The Essential Tools

The following are some essential tools for the beginner hardware hacker—someone who is curious about dabbling in and experimenting with simple hacks. It always helps to have a good stock of various equipment, wires, tools, components, and other materials in your workshop so you don't have to run out to the store every time you need something. Here are the basics:

- **Bright overhead lighting or desk lamp** Well-diffused overhead lighting is recommended—bright white fluorescent or incandescent bulbs serve this purpose. A smaller, high-intensity desk lamp will prove especially helpful for close-up work.
- **Protective gear** Mask or respirator, goggles, rubber gloves, smock or lab coat, earplugs. A sampling of protective gear is shown in Figure 1.1. Such gear should be worn at all times when performing your hacks. Use the respirator to prevent breathing in noxious fumes and fine dust from painting, cleaning, cutting, or soldering. The goggles protect your eyes from stray plastic or wood chips during drilling. Use the smock to prevent damage (burns and stains) to clothing.

Figure 1.1 Protective Gear

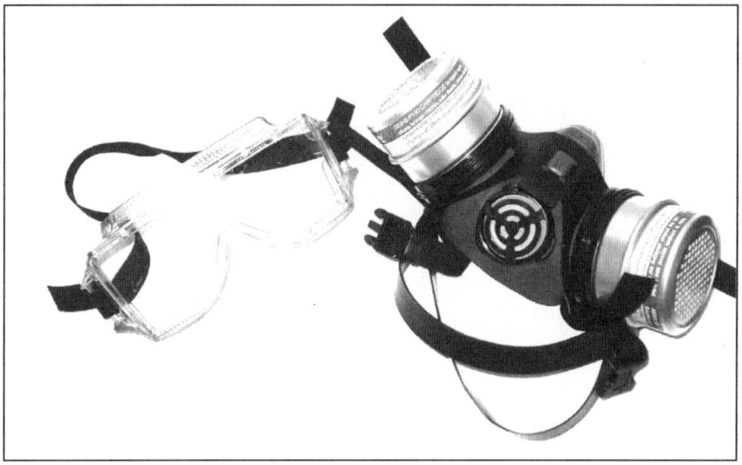

- **Electrostatic discharge (ESD) protection** If you live in a dry environment that is prone to static electricity, it is recommended that you purchase an antistatic mat and wrist strap from a local electronics store to prevent static discharge and protect sensitive electronic circuitry from getting damaged. Make sure the antistatic mat is properly grounded so that it can serve its intended purpose. Think of walking on a shag rug in your bare feet and then touching the radiator or a sibling. You'll feel ESD at work. However, ESD can damage components, even if you don't feel anything. You don't want that happening to the device you're hacking.

- **Screwdrivers** Regular-sized Phillips and flathead screwdrivers and a smaller set of jeweler's screwdrivers. The more sizes and types, the better, because you never know what sorts of hardware you'll want to open.
- **X-ACTO hobby knife** The modeling tool of choice for crafters, artists, and hobbyists. An essential general-purpose tool, especially useful for case mods and circuit board hacks. Over 50 different blade types are available.
- **Dremel tool** Extremely useful carving tool. Helpful for case mods and opening housings. Some models support rotation speeds from single-digit revolutions per second up to tens of thousands. Many various bit types (drilling, sanding, carving, engraving), accessories, and attachments are available. Example: Dremel 395 Variable-Speed MultiPro, $74.99 (see Figure 1.2).

Figure 1.2 Dremel Tool

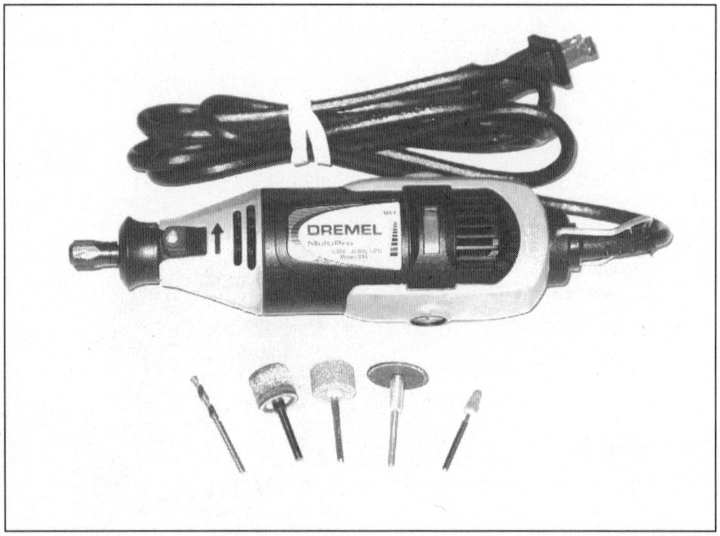

- **Needle file set** Designed for precise filing (see Figure 1.3). Ideal for deburring drilled holes and preparing modified surfaces. Most five-piece sets include square, flat, triangle, round, and elliptical files. Example: Radio Shack Kronus 5-Piece Needle File Set #64-2977, $7.99.
- **Tweezers** Handy for dealing with small components, holding wires, and pulling out splinters. There are dozens of tweezer styles, including long, extra long, flat tipped, curved, blunt, bent angle, medical, and surgical. The more variety you have in your toolkit, the better.

Figure 1.3 Needle File Set

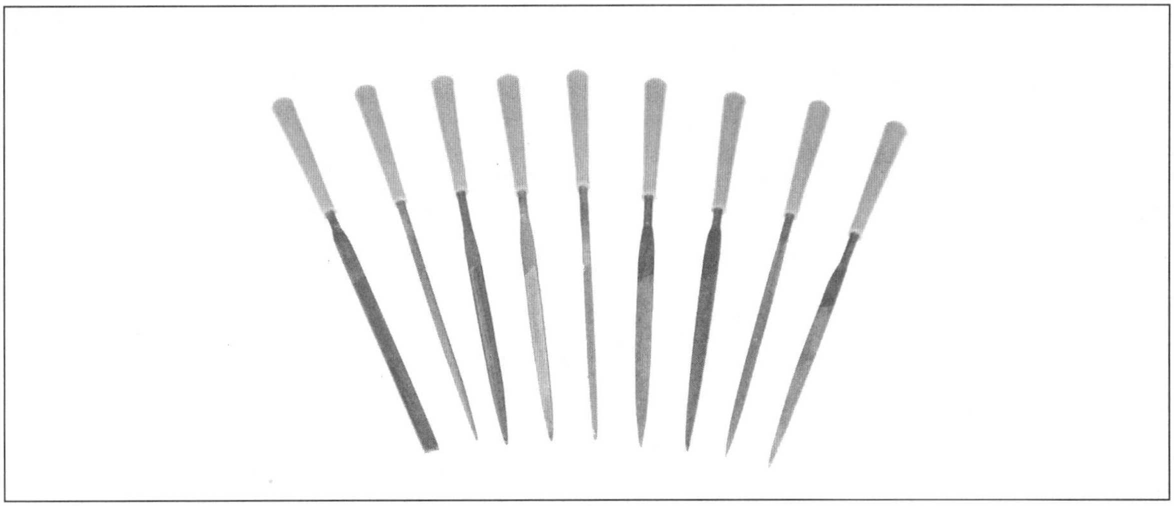

- **Wire brushes** Great for cleaning tough surfaces, especially metal. Useful for removing rust, dirt, and debris or preparing surfaces to be painted. It is recommended that you have a hand-sized brush for large areas and a smaller toothbrush-shaped brush for more detailed work.
- **Sandpaper** All-purpose sanding sheets are useful for removing dirt and debris, deburring edges, or preparing surfaces to be painted or glued together. An assortment of various grits (for example, 100, 220, 400, and 600) is recommended.
- **Glues** Wood glue, Gorilla Glue, Super Glue, epoxy, hot glue, acrylic cement. The more types of adhesive that you have on hand, the better off you'll be, because some glues work better on certain surfaces than others. A sampling of glues is shown in Figure 1.4.

Figure 1.4 Types of Glue

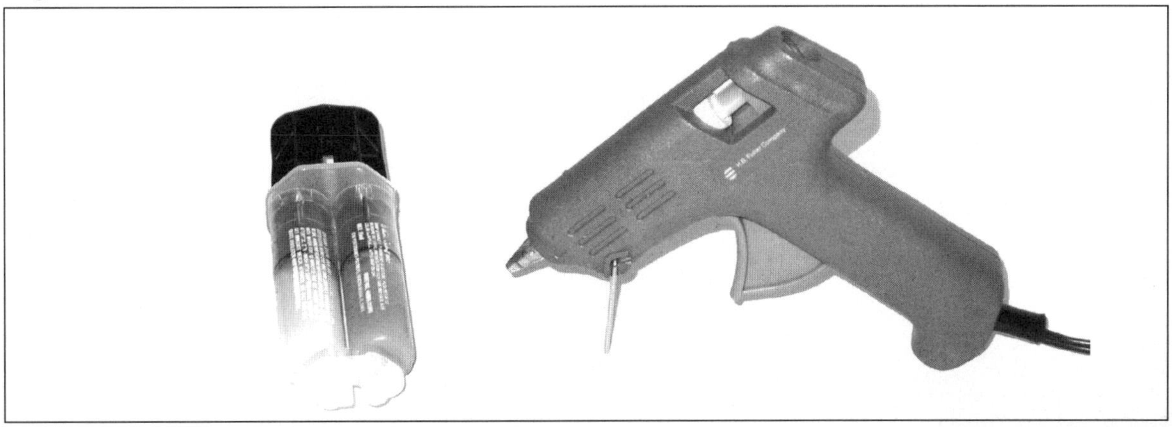

- **Tape** Duct tape, masking tape, electrical tape, Scotch/transparent tape, double-sided foam tape.
- **Cleaning supplies** A good workspace is a clean workspace. Typical cleaning supplies include cotton swabs, alcohol pads, paper towels, and some type of spray cleaning solution (for example, Fantastik).
- **Miscellaneous mechanical pieces** These are the standard hardware pieces that you'd find in any household workshop: nails, screws, stand-offs/spacers, washers, nuts, and bolts.

Basic Hardware Hacking

The following mid-range tools are what you'll need for more serious hardware hacking.

- **Variable-speed cordless drill** This is the essential multipurpose tool. It's especially useful for case mods. Example: Skil 18V Cordless Drill/Driver #2867 with 3/8-inch keyless chuck and six torque settings, $69.99 (see Figure 1.5).

Figure 1.5 Variable-Speed Cordless Drill

- **Drill bit set** What good is your variable-speed cordless drill without a complete set of drill bits of various sizes? Standard sizes include 1/16, 5/64, 3/32, 7/64, 1/8, 9/64, 5/32, 11/64, 3/16, 1/4, 7/32, 5/16, and 3/8 inch. Example: Black & Decker General Purpose 17-Piece Drill Bit Set, $18.95.

- **Security driver bit set** Security and tamper-resistant screws are sometimes used on product housings to prevent them from being easily opened. There are many types of these specially shaped bits (see Figure 1.6). To identify a particular bit type you might need to use for a hack, visit www.lara.com/reviews/screwtypes.htm.

Figure 1.6 Security Driver Bit Set

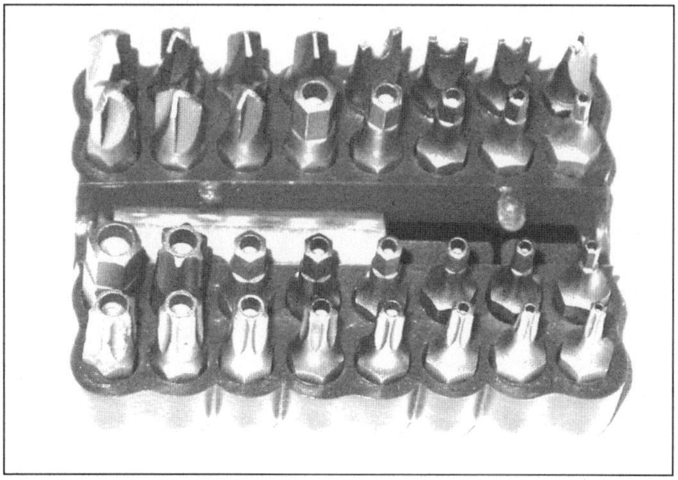

- **Heat gun and heat-shrink tubing** Heat guns look a lot like hair dryers, but, as many instructions thoughtfully point out, they should never be used for drying hair. Heat guns provide an extremely hot, directed flow of air through a nozzle (see Figure 1.7). They are commonly used for removing paint, melting glue, quickly drying surfaces, and shrinking heat-shrink tubing and plastic film. Basic heat guns have single temperature and airflow settings. More advanced models have multiple settings, giving you more control based on your intended application. Example: Milwaukee Dual Temperature Heat Gun (570 and 1000 degrees F), $69.95.

Figure 1.7 Heat Gun

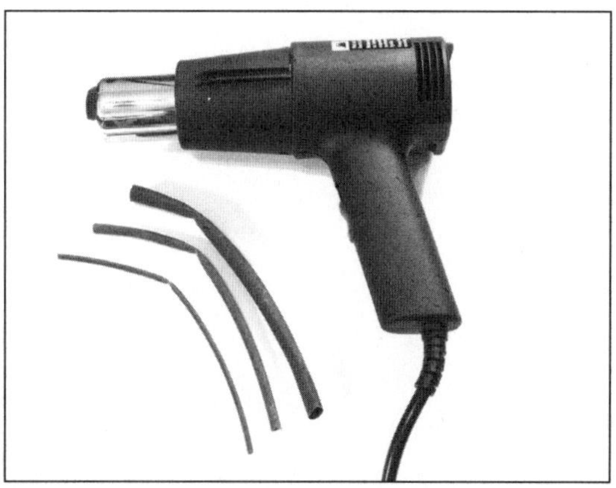

- **Center punch** Used to mark the target drill spot on a drilling surface, which will prevent the drill bit from slipping. Manual or automatic types exist. You could also use a permanent marker, but that won't stop your drill from slipping.
- **Nibbling tool** This tool "nibbles" away at light-gauge sheet metal, copper, aluminum, or plastic with each squeeze of the handle. Good for housing modifications and creating custom shapes. Example: Radio Shack Kronus Nibbling Tool #64-2960, $12.99 (see Figure 1.8).

Figure 1.8 Nibbling Tool

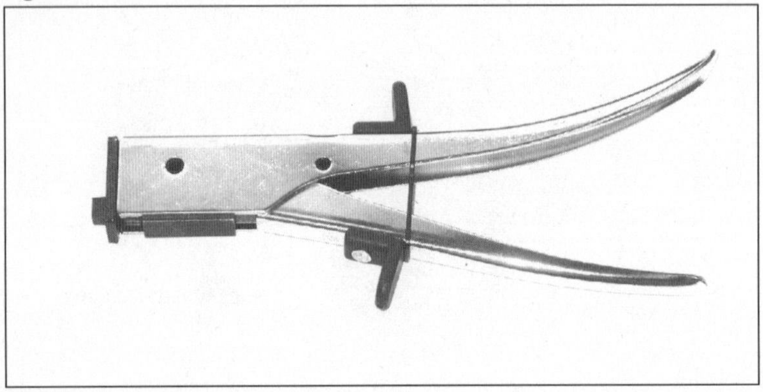

- **Jigsaw** Essential power tool for cutting and shaping. Useful for large pieces of material for which a smaller saw or drill isn't suitable. Example: Bosch 1587AVSK Top-Handle Jigsaw, $134.99.
- **Wire strippers** For cutting or stripping 10- to 22-AWG wire. Example: Radio Shack Kronus Gauged Wire Stripper #64-2980, $7.99 (see Figure 1.9).
- **Wire clippers** Example: Radio Shack Kronus 4.5-inch Mini Diagonal Cutters #64-2951, $4.99, or Radio Shack Kronus 5-inch Nippy Cutter #64-2959, $4.99 (see Figure 1.9).
- **Needle-nose pliers** Example: Radio Shack Kronus 6-inch Long-Nose Pliers #64-2954, $5.99 (see Figure 1.9).

Figure 1.9 Wire Strippers, Clippers, and Pliers

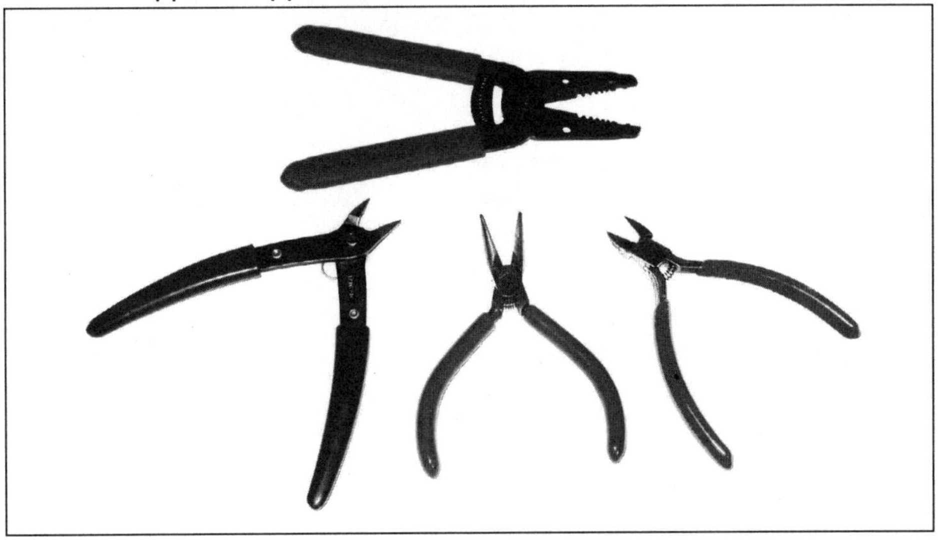

- **Soldering station** Soldering tools, ranging from a simple stick iron to a full-fledged rework station, come in many shapes and sizes (see Figure 1.10). More advanced models include adjustable temperature control, automatic shut-off, and interchangeable tips for various component package types and soldering needs. Recommended is a fine-tip, 700 degree F, 50W soldering stick iron. Approximate price range $10.00 to $1,000.00. Example: Weller W60P Controlled-Output Soldering Iron, $67.95.

Figure 1.10 Soldering Station

- **Soldering accessories** Essential soldering gear includes solder, no-clean flux, desoldering braid, vacuum desoldering tool (a.k.a. "solder sucker"), IC extraction tool, and ChipQuik

SMD removal kit. Solder should be thin gauge (0.032-inch or 0.025-inch diameter) 60/40 rosin core. The no-clean flux is used to provide good heat transfer between the iron and surfaces to be soldered. Flux often helps prevent cold solder joints, a common soldering problem. The desoldering tool is a manual vacuum device that pulls up hot solder, useful for removing components from circuit boards (Radio Shack #64-2098, $7.29). The IC extraction tool helps lift integrated circuits from the board during removal/desoldering (Radio Shack #276-1581, $8.39). The ChipQuik kit allows you to remove surface-mount components quickly and easily. Some soldering accessories are shown in Figure 1.11.

Figure 1.11 Soldering Accessories

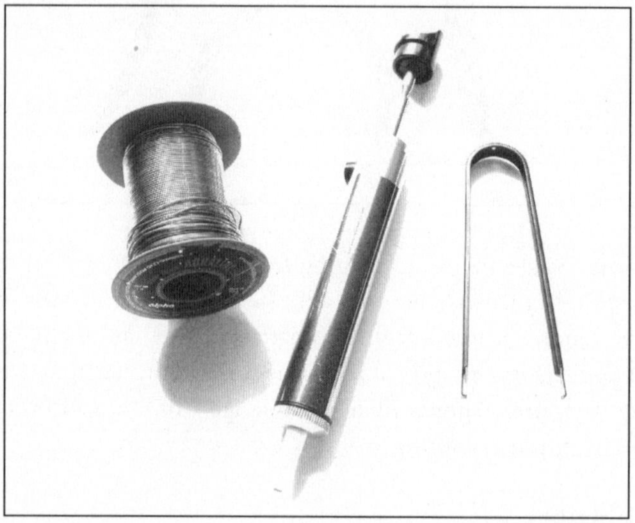

- **Basic electronic components** These include resistors, capacitors, diodes, transistors, light-emitting diodes (LEDs), and switches. It is useful to have a "junk bin" for all sorts of electronics bits and pieces. Old computer equipment and circuit boards are also useful because you can scavenge parts from them as needed. At a minimum, you should have a basic assortment of the most common values of components. Example: Digi-Key 1/4 Watt Resistor Assortment #RS125-ND, $14.95, and Digi-Key Miniature Electrolytic Capacitor Assortment #P835-KIT-ND, $29.95.
- **Miscellaneous wires and cables** This category includes cabling and wiring such as test leads, alligator clips, computer cables (USB, serial, parallel), and spools of wire (various colors and lengths, solid or stranded, 20–24AWG).

Advanced Projects and Reverse Engineering

The following tools are for the hardcore hardware hacker who is seriously dedicated to his or her trade. This equipment is mostly targeted toward reverse engineering of circuitry and for use in advanced electronic projects in which you might need to analyze part of a system or create your own circuits. More specific tools exist as well, but generally the tools in this section will get you as far as you need to go for a successful hardware hack of almost any type.

- **Digital multimeter (DMM)** Commonly referred to as the "Swiss army knife" of electronics measurement tools (see Figure 1.12), these are (usually) portable devices that provide a number of precision measurement functions, including AC/DC voltage, resistance, capacitance, current, and continuity. More advanced models also include frequency counters, graphical displays, and digital oscilloscope functionality. Reliable meters have high DC input resistance (also called *input impedance*) of at least 10Mohm. Approximate price range, $20.00 to $500.00. Example: Fluke Model 111, $129.00.

Figure 1.12 Digital Multimeter

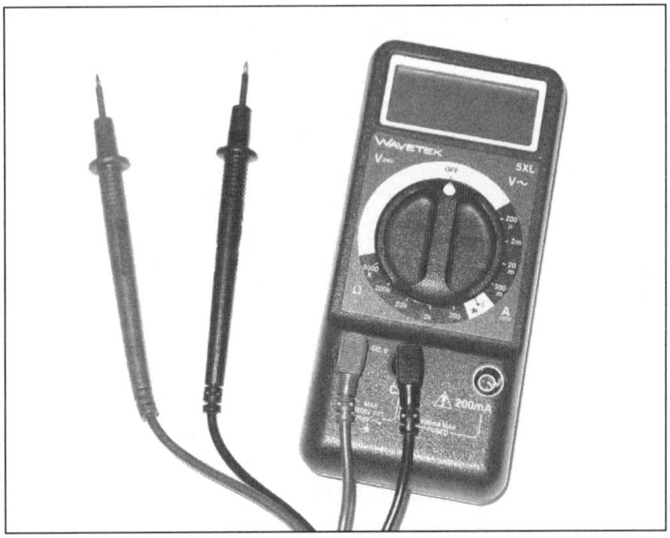

- **Analog multimeter** The older siblings to the DMM, these devices provide measurements of AC/DC voltage, resistance, current, and continuity on an analog meter display. Useful for showing slow variations or unusual wave shapes that a DMM may not be able to detect or recognize. Example: Radio Shack Analog Display Compact 8-Range Multimeter #22-218A, $15.49.
- **Adjustable power supply** Useful for any electronics-related design or hacking. Adjustable, linear, current-limited DC supply (see Figure 1.13). Current limiting often prevents parts from failing (burning up or exploding) when there is a short circuit.

Approximate price range, $100.00 to $1,000.00. Example: HP/Agilent Triple Output DC Power Supply E3630A, $588.00.

Figure 1.13 Adjustable Power Supply

- **Device programmer** Used to read and write memories (RAM, ROM, EPROM, EEPROM, Flash), microcontrollers, and programmable logic devices (see Figure 1.14). Extremely useful to extract program code and stored data. Approximate price range, $10.00 (home-built) to $2,500.00. Example: EE Tools' ChipMax, $345.00.

Figure 1.14 Device Programmer

- **UV EPROM eraser** This tool is used to erase UV-erasable EPROM devices in a matter of minutes using high-intensity ultraviolet light (see Figure 1.15). Approximate price range, $25.00 to $250.00. Example: Logical Devices Palm Erase, $59.95.

Figure 1.15 UV EPROM Eraser

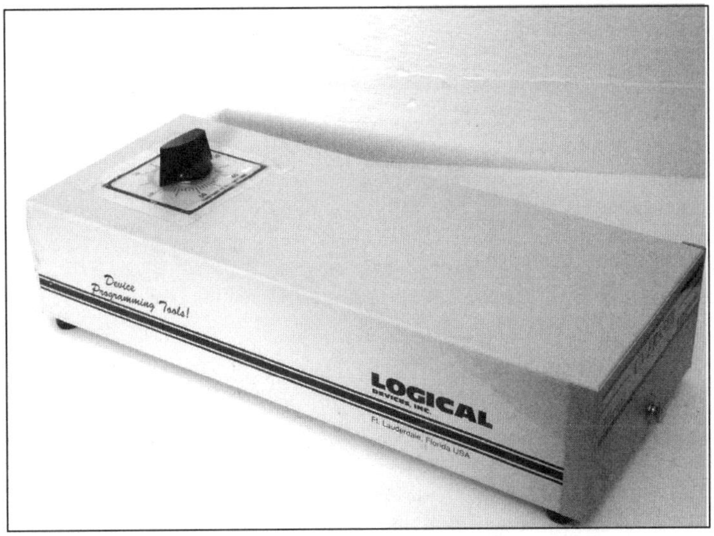

- **PCB etching kit** These kits are used to create printed circuit boards for custom hardware hacks. This process is time consuming and uses hazardous chemicals. Radio Shack provides a kit that contains two 3-inch by 4.5-inch copper-clad circuit boards, resist-ink pen, etching and stripping solutions, etching tank, 1/16-inch drill bit, polishing pad, and complete instructions. PCB etching materials can also be purchased separately at most any electronics distributor. Example: Radio Shack PC Board Kit #276-1576, $15.49.
- **Oscilloscope** Arguably the most important of advanced measurement tools, this provides a visual display of electrical signals and how they change over time (see Figure 1.16). Available in analog, digital, and mixed-mode versions. Previously owned analog oscilloscopes are typically the most economical and are available at many surplus electronics stores. Look for a bandwidth of greater than 50MHz. Approximate price range, $100.00 (used) to $10,000.00. Example: Tektronix 475A 250MHz Analog, $250.00, or Tektronix TDS3034B 4-Channel 300MHz Color Digital Storage, $6,795.00.

Figure 1.16 Oscilloscope

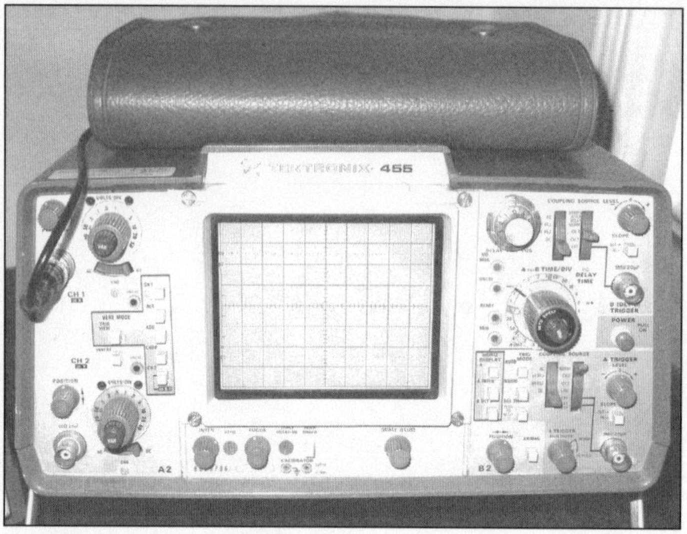

- **Logic analyzer** An advanced measurement tool useful for concurrently capturing large quantities of digital data from multiple sources. Primarily used for debugging address and data bus access and complex digital circuits. A logic analyzer is characterized by the number of digital samples it can sample at once, the maximum sampling rate, and the maximum sampling depth. Other features include glitch detection, programmable trigger algorithms, and protocol decoding/analysis. Newer systems typically use Windows CE or Windows XP Embedded. Previously owned logic analyzers are the most economical and suitable for most any development or hardware hacking lab—even the "low-end" models serve as excellent diagnostic tools. Approximate price range, $1,000.00 (used) to $50,000. Example: Hewlett-Packard 1661A, $1,695.00 (used; see Figure 1.17).

Where to Obtain the Tools

This short list of manufacturers and distributors will get you started in finding the supplies you need. The hacks on the DVD list more specific outlets for each particular type of hardware hack. Your local hardware store, art supply store, hobby shop, or electronic surplus store could also have some useful equipment for you.

Figure 1.17 Logic Analyzer

- The Home Depot, well-known nationwide hardware and home-remodeling chain, www.homedepot.com
- Lowe's, another nationwide hardware and home improvement chain, www.lowes.com
- Hobby Lobby, the nation's largest and most complete creative center; over 60,000 items of arts and crafts supplies, www.hobbylobby.com
- McMaster-Carr, the leading supplier of all things mechanical, including nuts, bolts, washers, lighting, fasteners, hand tools, and raw materials such as metal, ceramic, rubber, plastic, felt, and glass; over 400,000 products to choose from, and 98 percent of those are in stock, www.mcmaster.com
- Radio Shack, well-known supplier of electronic tools, components, and various consumer electronics, www.radioshack.com
- Digi-Key, major distributor for thousands of electronic components, www.digikey.com
- Contact East, leading product distributor for engineering tools, equipment, and materials, www.contacteast.com
- Test Equity, specializing in the sale and rental of used electronic test/measurement equipment, www.testequity.com

Chapter 2

Electrical Engineering Basics

Topics in this chapter:

- Introduction
- Fundamentals
- Basic Device Theory
- Soldering Techniques
- Common Engineering Mistakes
- Web Links and Other Resources

Note: Not all hacks on the DVD require electrical engineering.

Introduction

Understanding how hardware hacks work usually requires an introductory-level knowledge of electronics. This chapter describes electronics fundamentals and the basic theory of the most common electronic components. We also look at how to read schematic diagrams, how to identify components, proper soldering techniques, and other engineering topics.

NEED TO KNOW...LIMITATIONS OF THIS CHAPTER

Engineering, like hardware hacking, is a skill that requires time and determination if you want to be proficient in the field. There is a lot to discuss, but we have a limited amount of space. This chapter is not going to turn you into an electronics guru, but it will teach you enough about the basics so that you can start to find your way around. For more detail on the subject, see the suggested reading list at the end of this chapter.

Fundamentals

It is important to understand the core fundamentals of electronics before you venture into the details of specific components. This section provides a background on numbering systems, notation, and basic theory used in all facets of engineering.

Bits, Bytes, and Nibbles

At the lowest level, electronic circuits and computers store information in binary format, which is a base-2 numbering system containing only 0 and 1, each known as a *bit* (derived from a combination of the words *binary*, which is defined as something having two parts or components, and *digit*). The common decimal numbering system that we use in everyday life is a base-10 system, which consists of the digits 0 through 9.

Electrically, a 1 bit is generally represented by a positive voltage (5V, for example), and a 0 bit is generally represented by a zero voltage (or ground potential). However, many protocols and definitions map the binary values in different ways.

A group of 4 bits is a *nibble* (also known as a *nybble*), a group of 8 bits is a *byte*, and a group of 16 bits is typically defined as a *word* (though a *word* is sometimes defined differently, depending on the system architecture you are referring to). Figure 2.1 shows the interaction of bits, nibbles, bytes, and words. This visual diagram makes it easy to grasp the concept of how they all fit together.

Figure 2.1 Breakdown of a 16-Bit Word into Bytes, Nibbles, and Bits

<table>
<tr><td colspan="16">Word</td></tr>
<tr><td colspan="8">Byte 1 (High)</td><td colspan="8">Byte 0 (Low)</td></tr>
<tr><td colspan="4">Nibble 3</td><td colspan="4">Nibble 2</td><td colspan="4">Nibble 1</td><td colspan="4">Nibble 0</td></tr>
<tr><td>Bit 15</td><td>Bit 14</td><td>Bit 13</td><td>Bit 12</td><td>Bit 11</td><td>Bit 10</td><td>Bit 9</td><td>Bit 8</td><td>Bit 7</td><td>Bit 6</td><td>Bit 5</td><td>Bit 4</td><td>Bit 3</td><td>Bit 2</td><td>Bit 1</td><td>Bit 0</td></tr>
</table>

The larger the group of bits, the more information that can be represented. A single bit can represent only two combinations (0 or 1). A nibble can represent 2^4 (or 16) possible combinations (0 to 15 in decimal), a byte can represent 2^8 (or 256) possible combinations (0 to 255 in decimal), and a word can represent 2^{16} (or 65,536) possible combinations (0 to 65,535 in decimal).

Hexadecimal format, also called *hex*, is commonly used in the digital computing world to represent groups of binary digits. It is a base-16 system in which 16 sequential numbers are used as base units before adding a new position for the next number (digits 0 through 9 and letters A through F). One hex digit can represent the arrangement of 4 bits (a nibble). Two hex digits can represent 8 bits (a byte). Table 2.1 shows equivalent number values in the decimal, hexadecimal, and binary number systems. Hex digits are sometimes prefixed with 0x or $ to avoid confusion with other numbering systems.

Table 2.1 Number System Equivalents: Decimal, Binary, and Hexadecimal

Decimal	Binary	Hex
0	0	0
1	1	1
2	10	2
3	11	3
4	100	4
5	101	5
6	110	6
7	111	7
8	1000	8
9	1001	9

Continued

Table 2.1 continued Number System Equivalents: Decimal, Binary, and Hexadecimal

Decimal	Binary	Hex
10	1010	A
11	1011	B
12	1100	C
13	1101	D
14	1110	E
15	1111	F
16	10000	10
17	10001	11
18	10010	12
19	10011	13
20	10100	14
21	10101	15
22	10110	16
23	10111	17
24	11000	18
25	11001	19
26	11010	1A
27	11011	1B
28	11100	1C
29	11101	1D
30	11110	1E
31	11111	1F
32	100000	20
...	...	...
63	111111	3F
...	...	...
127	1111111	7F
...	...	...
255	11111111	FF

The American Standard Code for Information Interchange, or ASCII (pronounced *ask-key*), is the common code for storing characters in a computer system. The standard ASCII character set (see Table 2.2) uses 1 byte to correspond to each of 128 different letters, numbers, punctuation marks, and special characters. Many of the special characters are holdovers from the original specification created in 1968 and are no longer commonly used for their originally intended purpose. Only the decimal values 0 through 127 are assigned, which is half of the space available in a byte. An extended ASCII character set uses the full range of 256 characters available in a byte. The decimal values of 128 through 255 are assigned to represent other special characters that are used in foreign languages, graphics, and mathematics.

Table 2.2 The Standard ASCII Character Set

Hex	Symbol	Hex	Symbol	Hex	Symbol	Hex	Symbol
0x00	NUL (null)	0x20	SP (space)	0x40	@	0x60	' (Single quote)
0x01	SOH (start of heading)	0x21	!	0x41	A	0x61	a
0x02	STX (start of text)	0x22	"	0x42	B	0x62	b
0x03	ETX (end of text)	0x23	#	0x43	C	0x63	c
0x04	EOT (end of transmission)	0x24	$	0x44	D	0x64	d
0x05	ENQ (enquiry)	0x25	%	0x45	E	0x65	e
0x06	ACK (acknowledge)	0x26	&	0x46	F	0x66	f
0x07	BEL (bell)	0x27	' (apostrophe)	0x47	G	0x67	g
0x08	BS (backspace)	0x28	(	0x48	H	0x68	h
0x09	HT (horizontal tab)	0x29	)	0x49	I	0x69	i
0x0A	LF (line feed/new line)	0x2A	*	0x4A	J	0x6A	j
0x0B	VT (vertical tab)	0x2B	+	0x4B	K	0x6B	k
0x0C	FF (form feed)	0x2C	, (comma)	0x4C	L	0x6C	l
0x0D	CR (carriage return)	0x2D	-	0x4D	M	0x6D	m
0x0E	SO (shift out)	0x2E	. (period)	0x4E	N	0x6E	n
0x0F	SI (shift in)	0x2F	/	0x4F	O	0x6F	o
0x10	DLE (data link escape)	0x30	0	0x50	P	0x70	p
0x11	DC1 (device control 1)	0x31	1	0x51	Q	0x71	q
0x12	DC2 (device control 2)	0x32	2	0x52	R	0x72	r
0x13	DC3 (device control 3)	0x33	3	0x53	S	0x73	s
0x14	DC4 (device control 4)	0x34	4	0x54	T	0x74	t
0x15	NAK (negative acknowledge)	0x35	5	0x55	U	0x75	u
0x16	SYN (synchronous idle)	0x36	6	0x56	V	0x76	v
0x17	ETB (end of transmission block)	0x37	7	0x57	W	0x77	w
0x18	CAN (cancel)	0x38	8	0x58	X	0x78	x
0x19	EM (end of medium)	0x39	9	0x59	Y	0x79	y
0x1A	SUB (substitute)	0x3A	: (colon)	0x5A	Z	0x7A	z

Continued

Table 2.2 continued The Standard ASCII Character Set

Hex	Symbol	Hex	Symbol	Hex	Symbol	Hex	Symbol
0x1B	ESC (escape)	0x3B	;	0x5B	[	0x7B	{
0x1C	FS (file separator)	0x3C	<	0x5C	\	0x7C	|
0x1D	GS (group separator)	0x3D	=	0x5D	]	0x7D	}
0x1E	RS (record separator)	0x3E	>	0x5E	^	0x7E	~
0x1F	US (unit separator)	0x3F	?	0x5F	_ (underscore)	0x7F	Del (delete)

Reading Schematics

Before we get into the theory of individual electronic components, it is important to learn how circuit designs are drawn and described. A *schematic* is essentially an electrical road map of a circuit. Reading basic schematics is a good skill to have, even if it is just to identify a particular component that needs to be removed during a hack. Reading schematics is much easier than it may appear, and with practice it will become second nature.

On a schematic, each component of the circuit is assigned its own symbol, unique to the type of device that it is. The United States and Europe sometimes use different symbols, and there are even multiple symbols to represent one type of part. A resistor has its own special symbol, as does a capacitor, a diode, or an integrated circuit. Think of schematic symbols as an alphabet for electronics. Table 2.3 shows a selection of basic components and their corresponding designators and schematic symbols. This is by no means a complete list, and, as mentioned, a particular component type may have additional symbols that aren't shown here.

A *part designator* is also assigned to each component and is used to distinguish between two parts of the same type and value. The designator is usually an alphanumeric character followed by a unique numerical value (R1, C4, or SW2, for example). The part designator and schematic symbol are used as a pair to define each discrete component of the circuit design.

Table 2.3 Designator and Schematic Symbols for Basic Electronic Components

Component	Designator	Symbol
Resistor	R	
Potentiometer (variable resistor)	R	
Capacitor (nonpolarized)	C	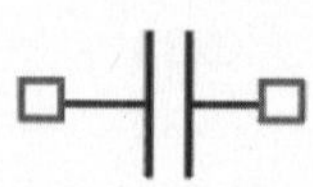

Continued

Table 2.3 continued Designator and Schematic Symbols for Basic Electronic Components

Component	Designator	Symbol
Capacitor (polarized)	C	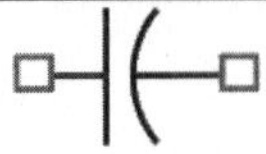
Diode	D	
LED	D	
Photodiode	D	
Transistor (NPN)	Q	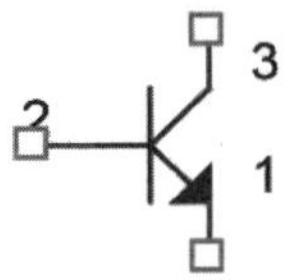
Transistor (PNP)	Q	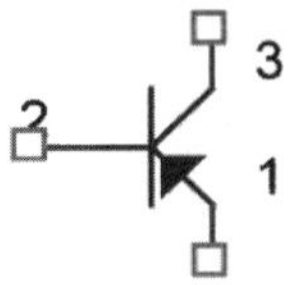
Crystal	Y	
Switch	SW	
Pushbutton switch	SW	
Speaker	LS	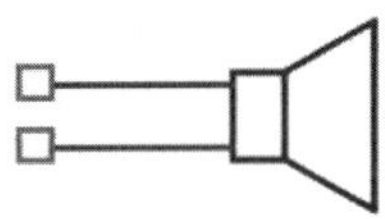
Fuse	F	
Battery	BT	

Continued

Table 2.3 continued Designator and Schematic Symbols for Basic Electronic Components

Component	Designator	Symbol
	None	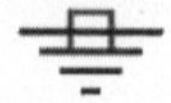
Ground	None	
	None	

Figure 2.2 An Example Circuit: A Basic LED with a Current-Limiting Resistor and Switch

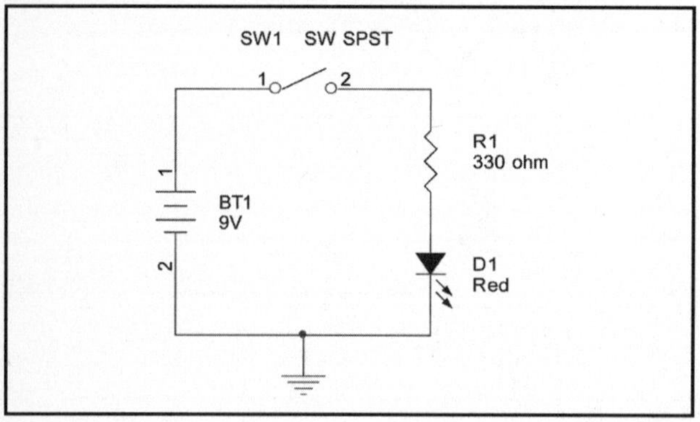

Figure 2.2 shows an example circuit using some of the basic schematic symbols. It describes a light-emitting diode (LED) powered by a battery and controlled by a switch. When the switch is off, no current is able to flow from the battery through the rest of the circuit, so the LED will not illuminate. When the switch is enabled, current will flow and the LED will illuminate.

Voltage, Current, and Resistance

Voltage and current are the two staple quantities of electronics. *Voltage*, also known as a *potential difference*, is the amount of work (energy) required to move a positive charge from a lower potential (a more negative point in a circuit) to higher potential (a more positive point in a circuit). Voltage can be thought of as an electrical pressure or force and has a unit of volts (*V*). It is denoted with a symbol *V*, or sometimes *E* or *U*.

Current is the rate of flow (the quantity of electrons) passing through a given point. Current has a unit of amperes, or *amps* (*A*), and is denoted with a symbol of *I*. Kirchhoff's Current Law states that the sum of currents into a point equals the sum of the currents out of a point (corresponding to a conservation of charge).

Power is a "snapshot" of the amount of work being done at that particular point in time and has a unit of watts (W). One watt of power is equal to the work done in 1 second by 1 volt moving 1 coulomb of charge. Furthermore, 1 coulomb per second is equal to 1 ampere. A coulomb is equal to

6.25 x 10^{18} electrons (a very, very large amount). Basically, the power consumed by a circuit can be calculated with the following simple formula:

P = V x I

where

- P = Power (W)
- V = Voltage (V)
- I = Current (A)

Need to Know… Differentiating Between Voltage and Current

We use special terminology to describe voltage and current. You should refer to voltage as going *between* or *across* two points in a circuit—for example, "The voltage across the resistor is 1.7V." You should refer to current going *through* a device or connection in a circuit—for example, "The current through the diode is 800mA." When we're measuring or referring to a voltage at a single given point in a circuit, it is defined with respect to ground (typically 0V).

Direct Current and Alternating Current

Direct current (DC) is simple to describe because it flows in one direction through a conductor and is either a steady signal or pulses. The most familiar form of a DC supply is a battery. Generally, aside from power supply or motor circuitry, DC voltages are more commonly used in electronic circuits.

Alternating current (AC) flows in both directions through a conductor (see Figure 2.3) and is arguably more difficult to analyze and work with than DC. The most familiar form of an AC supply is an electrical outlet in your home. In the United States and Canada, these outlets provide 120V AC at 60Hz (cycles per second). In other parts of the world, varying AC voltages and line frequencies are used.

Several terms are used to describe the AC signal:

- **Peak voltage (V_{PEAK})** The maximum positive and negative points of the AC signal from a center point of reference.

Figure 2.3 An Example of an Alternating Current Waveform

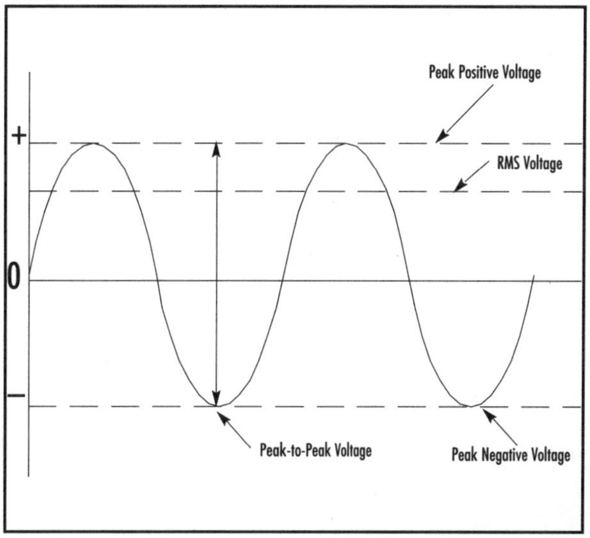

- **Peak-to-peak voltage (V_{PP})** The total voltage swing from the most positive to the most negative point of the AC signal.
- **Root-mean-square (RMS) voltage (V_{RMS})** The most common term used to describe an AC voltage. Since an AC signal is constantly changing (as opposed to DC, in which the signal is constant), the RMS measurement is the most accurate way to determine how much work will be done by an AC voltage.

For a typical sinusoidal AC signal (like the one shown in Figure 2.3), the following four formulas can be used:

Average AC Voltage (V_{AVG}) $= 0.637 \times V_{PEAK} = 0.9 \times V_{RMS}$

$V_{PEAK} = 1.414 \times V_{RMS} = 1.57 \times V_{AVG}$

$V_{RMS} = 0.707 \times V_{PEAK} = 1.11 \times V_{AVG}$

$V_{PP} = 2 \times V_{PEAK}$

Resistance

Resistance can be described with a simple analogy of water flowing through a pipe: If the pipe is narrow (high resistance), the flow of water (current) will be restricted. If the pipe is large (low resistance), water (current) can flow through it more easily. If the pressure (voltage) is increased, more current will be forced through the conductor. Any current prevented from flowing (if the resistance is high, for example) will be dissipated as heat (based on the first law of thermodynamics, which states that energy cannot be created or destroyed, simply changed in form). Additionally, there will be a difference in voltage on either side of the conductor.

Resistance is an important electrical property and exists in any electrical device. *Resistors* are devices used to create a fixed value of resistance. (For more information on resistors, see the "Basic Device Theory" section in this chapter.)

Ohm's Law

Ohm's Law, proven in the early 19th century by George Simon Ohm, is a basic formula of electronics that states the relationship among voltage, current, and resistance in an ideal conductor. The current in a circuit is directly proportional to the applied voltage and inversely proportional to the circuit resistance. Ohm's Law can be expressed as the following equations:

$V = I \times R$

Or...

$I = V / R$

Or...

$R = V / I$

Where...

- V = Voltage (V)
- I = Current (A)
- R = Resistance (in ohms, designated with the omega symbol, Ω)

Basic Device Theory

This section explores the basic device theory of the five most common electronic components: resistors, capacitors, diodes, transistors, and integrated circuits. Understanding the functionality of these parts is essential to any core electronics knowledge and will prove useful in designing or reverse-engineering products.

Resistors

Resistors are used to reduce the amount of current flowing through a point in a system. Resistors are defined by three values:

- Resistance (Ω)
- Heat dissipation (in watts, W)
- Manufacturing tolerance (%)

Figure 2.4 Various Resistor Types

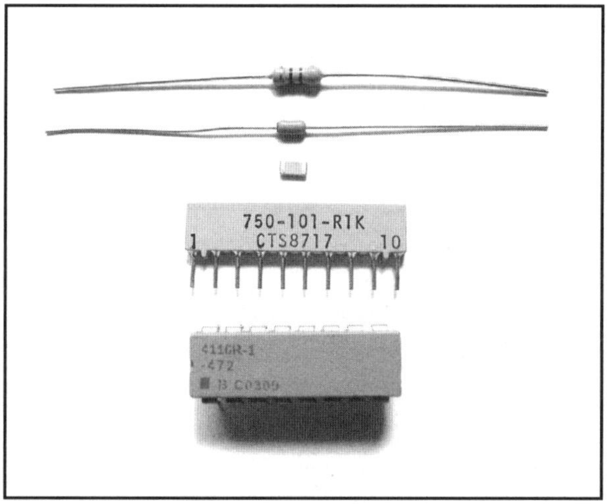

A sampling of various resistor types is shown in Figure 2.4. Resistors are not polarized, meaning that they can be inserted in either orientation with no change in electrical function.

The value of a resistor is indicated by an industry-standard code of four or five colored bands printed directly onto the resistor (see Figure 2.5). The bands define the resistance, multiplier, and manufacturing tolerance of the resistor. The manufacturing tolerance is the allowable skew of a resistor value from its ideal rated value.

A resistor's internal composition can consist of many different materials, but typically one of three are used: carbon, metal film, or wire-wound. The material is usually wrapped around a core, with the wrapping type and length corresponding to the resistor value. The carbon-filled resistor, used in most general-purpose applications such as current limiting and nonprecise circuits, allows a +/-5 % tolerance on the resistor value. Metal film resistors are for more precise applications such as amplifiers, power supplies, and sensitive analog circuitry; they usually allow a +/-1 or 2 % tolerance. Wire-wound resistors can also be very accurate.

When resistors are used in series in a circuit (see Figure 2.6), their resistance values are *additive*, meaning that you simply add the values of the resistors in series to obtain the total resistance. For example, if *R1* is 220 ohm and *R2* is 470 ohm, the overall resistance will be 690 ohm.

Parallel circuits provide alternative pathways for current flow, although the voltage across the components in parallel is the same. When resistors are used in parallel (see Figure 2.7), a simple equation is used to calculate the overall resistance:

$$1 / R_{TOTAL} = (1 / R1) + (1 / R2) + \dots$$

This same formula can be extended for any number of resistors used in parallel. For example, if *R1* is 220 ohm and *R2* is 470 ohm, the overall resistance will be 149.8 ohm.

For only two resistors in parallel, an alternate formula can be used:

$$R_{TOTAL} = (R1 \times R2) / (R1 + R2)$$

Figure 2.5 Resistor Color Code Chart

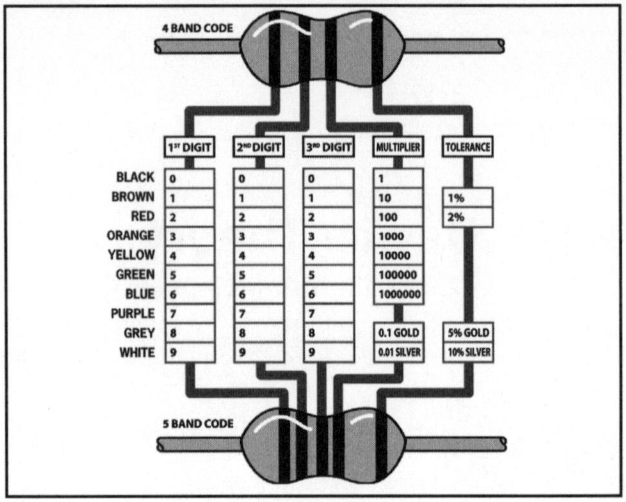

Figure 2.6 Resistors in Series

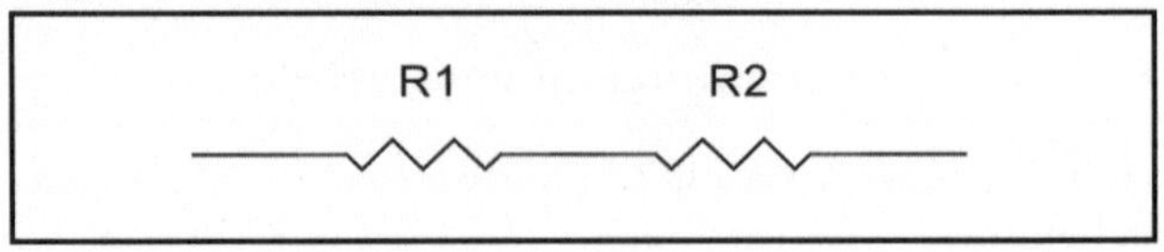

Figure 2.7 Resistors in Parallel

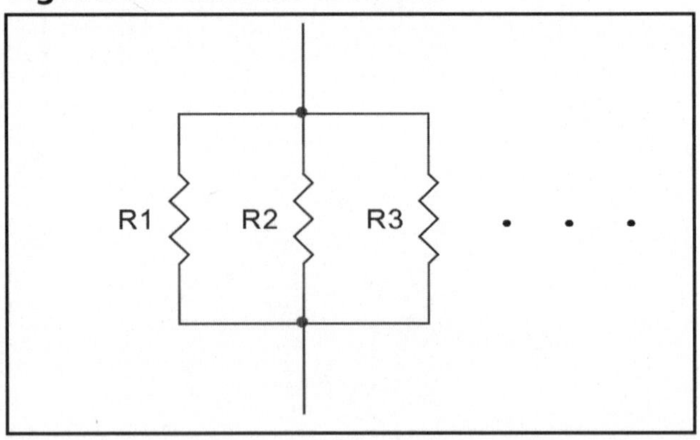

Carbon and metal film resistors typically come in wattage values of 1/16W, 1/8W, 1/4W, 1/2W and 1W. This corresponds to how much power they can safely dissipate. The most commonly used resistors are 1/4W and 1/2W. For large current applications, wire-wound resistors are typically used because they can support wattages greater than 1W. The wattage of the resistor usually corresponds to its physical size and surface area. For most consumer electronics, resistors greater than 1W are typically not used. To calculate the required wattage value for your application, use the following equation:

$$P = V \times I$$

Or...

$$P = I^2 \times R$$

Where...

- P = Power (W)
- V = Voltage across the resistor (V)
- I = Current flowing through the resistor (A)
- R = Resistance value (Ω)

Capacitors

A *capacitor's* primary function is to store electrical energy in the form of electrostatic charge. Consider a simple example of a water tower, which stores water (charge): When the water system (circuit) produces more water than a town or building needs, the excess is stored in the water tower (capacitor). At times of high demand, when additional water is needed, the excess water (charge) flows out of the water tower to keep the pressure up.

A capacitor is usually implemented for one of three uses:

- **To store a charge** Typically used for high-speed or high-power applications, such as a laser or a camera flash. The capacitor will be fully charged by the circuit in a fixed length of time, and then all of its stored energy will be released and used almost instantaneously, just like the water tower example previously described.
- **To block DC voltage** If a DC voltage source is connected in series to a capacitor, the capacitor will instantaneously charge and no DC voltage will pass into the rest of the circuit. However, an AC signal flows through a capacitor unimpeded because the capacitor will charge and discharge as the AC fluctuates, making it appear that the alternating current is flowing.
- **To eliminate ripples** Useful for filtering, signal processing, and other analog designs. If a line carrying DC voltage has ripples or spikes in it, also known as "noise," a capacitor can smooth or "clean" the voltage to a more steady value by absorbing the peaks and filling in the valleys of the noisy DC signal.

Capacitors are constructed of two metal plates separated by a *dielectric*. The dielectric is any material that does not conduct electricity, and varies for different types of capacitors. It prevents the plates from touching each other. Electrons are stored on one plate of the capacitor and they discharge through the other. Consider lightning in the sky as a real-world example of a capacitor: One plate is formed by the clouds, the other plate is formed by the earth's ground, and the dielectric is the air in between. The lightning is the charge releasing between the two plates.

Depending on their construction, capacitors are either *polarized*, meaning that they exhibit varying characteristics based on the direction they are used in a circuit, or *nonpolarized*, meaning that they can be inserted in either orientation with no change in electrical function. A sampling of various capacitor types is shown in Figures 2.8 and 2.9.

Figure 2.8 Various Nonpolarized Capacitor Types (Ceramic Disc and Multilayer)

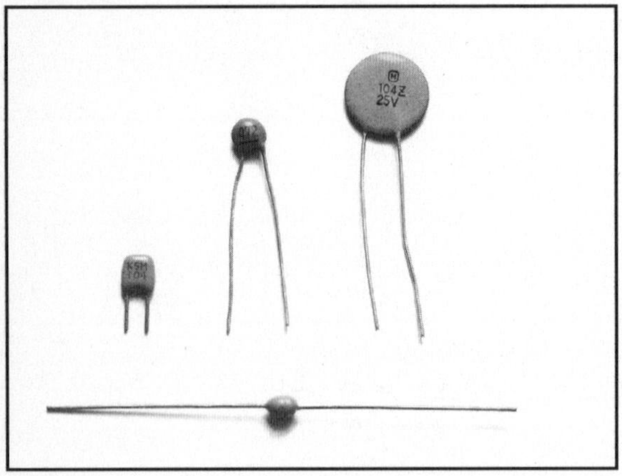

Figure 2.9 Various Polarized Capacitor Types (Electrolytic and Tantalum)

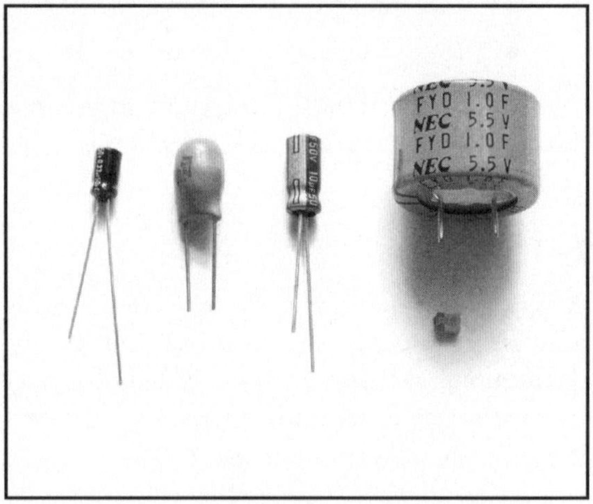

Capacitors have a unit of farad (F). A 1 farad capacitor can store 1 coulomb of charge at 1 volt (equal to 1 amp-second of electrons at 1 volt). A single farad is a very large amount. Most capacitors store a miniscule amount of charge and are usually denoted in uF (microfarads, 10^{-6} x F) or pF (picofarads, 10^{-12} x F). The physical size of the capacitor is usually related to the dielectric material and the amount of charge that the capacitor can hold.

Unlike resistors, capacitors do not use a color code for value identification. Today, most monolithic and ceramic capacitors are marked with a three-number code called an *IEC marking* (see Figure 2.10). The first two digits of the code indicate a numerical value; the last digit indicates a multiplier. Electrolytic capacitors are always marked in uF. These devices are polarized and must be oriented correctly during installation. Polarized devices have a visible marking denoting the negative side of the device (in the case of surface-mount capacitors, the marking is on the positive side). There may be additional markings on the capacitor (sometimes just a single character); these usually denote the capacitor's voltage rating or manufacturer.

Figure 2.10 Examples of Some Capacitor IEC Markings

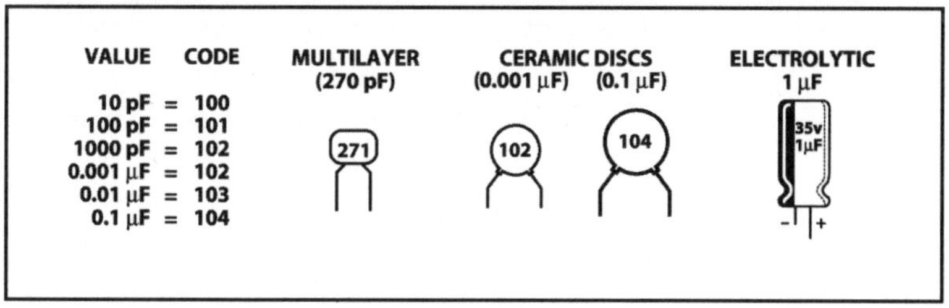

The calculations to determine effective capacitance of capacitors in series and parallel are essentially the reverse of those used for resistors. When capacitors are used in series (see Figure 2.11), a simple equation is used to calculate the effective capacitance:

$$1 / C_{TOTAL} = (1 / C1) + (1 / C2) + \ldots$$

This same formula can be extended for any number of capacitors used in series. For example, if *C1* is 100uF and *C2* is 47uF, the overall capacitance will be 31.9uF.

For only two capacitors in series, an alternate formula can be used:

$$C_{TOTAL} = (C1 \times C2) / (C1 + C2)$$

When using capacitors in series, you store effectively less charge than you would by using either one alone in the circuit. The advantage to capacitors in series is that it increases the maximum working voltage of the devices.

Figure 2.11 Capacitors in Series

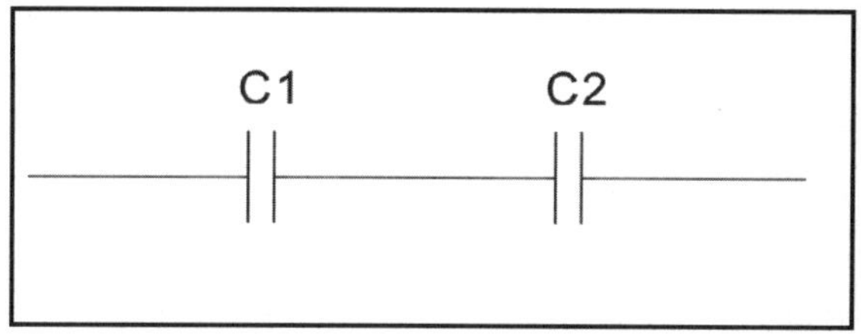

When capacitors are used in parallel in a circuit (see Figure 2.12), their effective capacitance is additive, meaning that you simply add the values of the capacitors in parallel to obtain the total capacitance. For example, if *C1* is 100uF and *C2* is 47uF, the overall capacitance will be 147uF.

Figure 2.12 Capacitors in Parallel

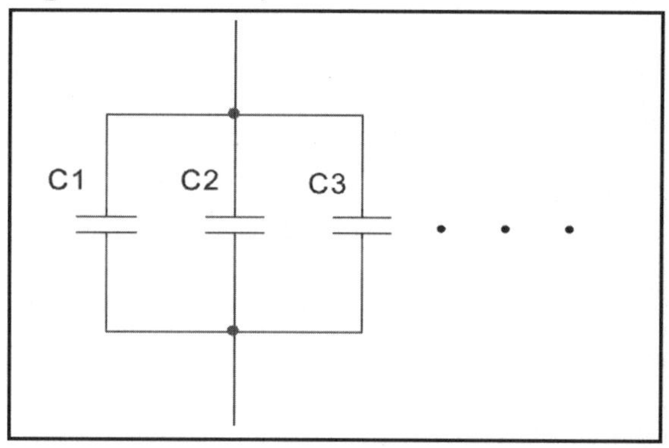

Capacitors are often used in combination with resistors in order to control their charge and discharge time. Resistance directly affects the time required to charge or discharge a capacitor (the larger the resistance, the longer the time).

Figure 2.13 shows a simple RC circuit. The capacitor will charge as shown by the curve in Figure 2.14. The amount of time for the capacitor to become fully charged in an RC circuit depends on the values of the capacitor and resistor in the circuit.

Figure 2.13 A Simple RC Circuit to Charge a Capacitor

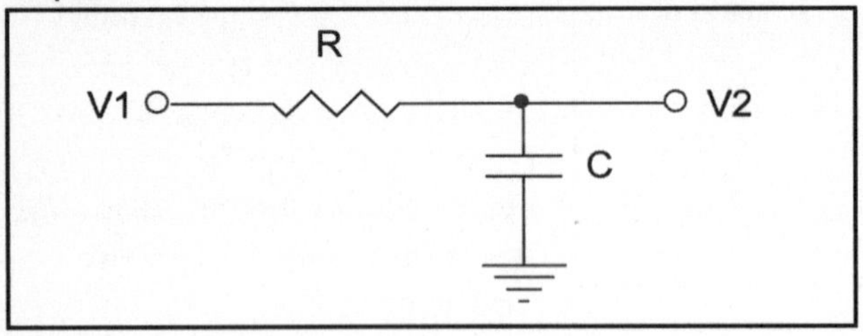

Figure 2.14 Capacitor-Charging Curve

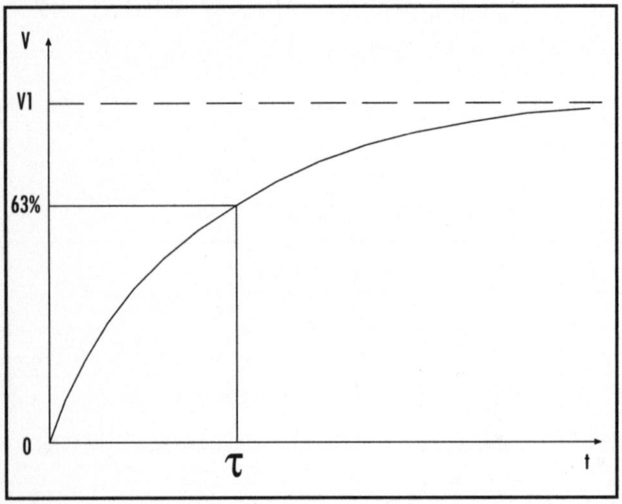

Figure 2.15 Various Diode Types Showing Direction of Current Flow

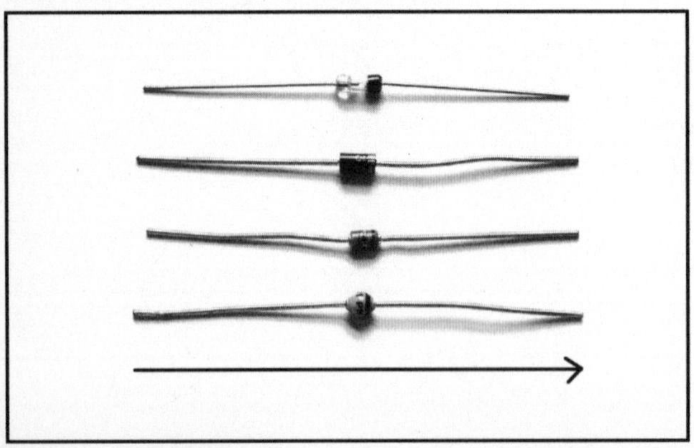

The variable τ (called the *time constant*) is used to define the time it takes for the capacitor to charge to 63.2 % of its maximum capacity. The time constant can be calculated by the following formula:

$$\tau = R \times C$$

Where...

- τ = Time constant (seconds)
- C = Capacitance (*F*)
- R = Resistance (Ω)

A capacitor reaches 63.2 % of its charge in one-fifth of the time it takes to become fully charged. Capacitors in actual applications are usually not charged to their full capacity because it takes too long.

Diodes

In the most basic sense, *diodes* pass current in one direction while blocking it from the other. This allows for their use in rectifying AC into DC, filtering, limiting the range of a signal (known as a *diode clamp*), and as "steering diodes," in which diodes are used to allow voltage to be applied to only one part of the circuit.

Most diodes are made with semiconductor materials such as silicon, germanium, or selenium. Diodes are polarized, meaning that they exhibit varying characteristics depending on the direction they are used in a circuit. When current is flowing through the diode in the direction shown in Figure 2.15 (from anode, left, to cathode, right), the diode appears as a short circuit. When current tries to pass in the opposite direction, the diode exhibits a high resistance, preventing the current from flowing.

Diodes come in many types and sizes, each with varying electrical properties. You need to consider characteristics such as breakdown voltage, forward voltage, forward current, and reverse recovery time when designing with diodes or replacing one in a circuit:

- **Breakdown/reverse voltage (V_R)**, also known as the *peak inverse voltage* (P_{IV}), is the maximum voltage you can apply across a diode in the reverse direction and still have it block conduction. If this voltage is exceeded, the diode goes into "avalanche breakdown" and conducts current, essentially rendering the diode useless (unless it's a Zener diode, which is designed to operate in this breakdown region).
- **Forward voltage (V_F)** is the voltage drop across the diode. This usually corresponds to the forward current (the greater the current flowing through the diode, the larger the voltage drop). Typical forward voltage of a general-purpose diode is between 0.5V and 0.8V at 10mA.
- **Forward current (I_F)** is the maximum current that can flow through the diode. If current flowing through the diode is more than it can handle, the diode will overheat and can melt down and cause a short circuit.
- **Reverse recovery time (T_{RR})** is the time it takes a diode to go from forward conduction to reverse blocking (think of a revolving door that goes in both directions and the people coming in and going out acting as the current). If the turnaround time is too slow, current will flow in the reverse direction when the polarity changes and cause the diode junction to heat up and possibly fail. This is primarily of concern for AC-rectifying circuits commonly used in power supplies.

Figure 2.16 The Diode V-I Curve

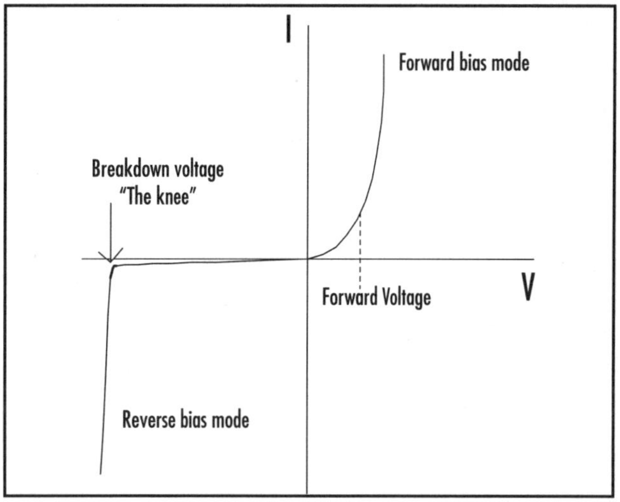

Figure 2.16 shows the diode V-I curve, a standard curve that describes the relationship between voltage and current with respect to a diode.

In normal forward bias operation (shown on the right side of the graph), the diode begins to conduct and act as a short circuit after the forward voltage drop is met (usually between 0.5V and 0.8V). In reverse bias operation (shown on the left side of the graph), reverse current is generally measured in the nA range (an extremely small measure of current). When the diode is reverse biased, current is essentially prevented from flowing in that direction, with the exception of a very small leakage current. The point at which the diode begins its avalanche breakdown is called "the knee," as shown by the visible increase in reverse current on the curve, looking somewhat similar to a profile of a knee. Breakdown is not a desirable mode to which to subject the diode, unless the diode is of a Zener type (in which case proper current limiting should be employed).

Transistors

The *transistor* is arguably the greatest invention of the 20th century and the most important of electronic components. It is a three-terminal device that essentially serves as an amplifier or switch to control electronic current. When a small current is applied to its base, a much larger current is allowed to flow from its collector. This gives a transistor its switching behavior, since a small current can turn a larger current on and off.

The first transistor was demonstrated on December 23, 1947, by William Shockley, John Bardeen, and Walter Brattain, all scientists at the Bell Telephone Laboratories in New Jersey. The transistor was the first device designed to act as both a transmitter, converting sound waves into electronic waves, and a resistor, controlling electronic current. The name *transistor* comes from the *trans* of *transmitter* and the *sistor* of *resistor*. Although its use has gone far beyond the function that combination implies, the name remains.

Figure 2.17 Various Discrete Transistor Types

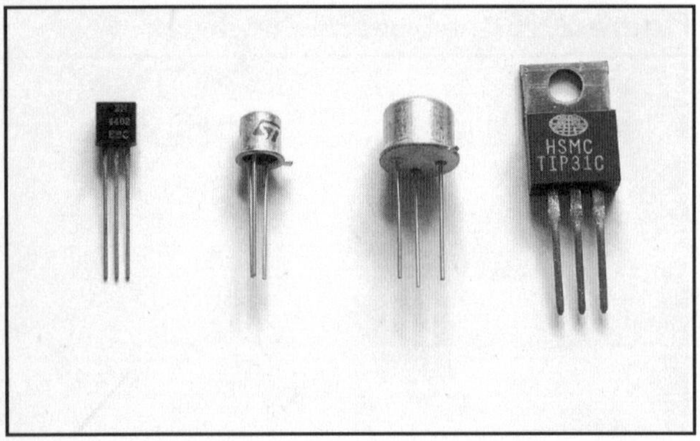

The transistor became commercially available on May 10, 1954, from Texas Instruments, and quickly replaced the bulky and unreliable vacuum tubes, which were much larger and required more power to operate. Jumping ahead 50 years, to 2004, transistors are now an essential part of engineering, used in practically every circuit and by the millions in single integrated circuits taking up an area smaller than a fingernail. Companies such as AMD, NEC, Samsung, and Intel are pushing the envelope of transistor technology, continuing to discover new ways to develop smaller, faster, and cheaper transistors.

This chapter only scratches the surface of transistor theory and focuses only on the most general terms. A sampling of various discrete transistors is shown in Figure 2.17.

The transistor is composed of a three-layer "sandwich" of semiconductor material. Depending on how the material's crystal structure is treated during its creation (in a process known as *doping*), it becomes more positively charged (P-type) or negatively charged (N-type). The transistor's three-layer structure contains a P-type layer between N-type layers (known as an NPN configuration) or an N-type layer sandwiched between P-type layers (known as a PNP configuration).

The voltages at a transistor terminal (*C* for the collector, *E* for the emitter, and *B* for the base) are measured with respect to ground and are identified by their pin names, V_C, V_E, and V_B, respectively. The voltage drop measured between two terminals on the transistor is indicated by a double-subscript (for example, V_{BE} corresponds to the voltage drop from the base to the emitter). Figure 2.18 shows the typical single NPN and PNP schematic symbols and notations.

A trick to help you remember which diagram corresponds to which transistor type is to think of NPN as meaning "not pointing in" (in reference to the base-emitter diode). With that said, the other transistor is obviously the PNP type.

An NPN transistor has four properties that must be met (the properties for the PNP type are the same, except the polarities are reversed):

1. The collector must be more positive than the emitter.
2. The base-emitter and base-collector circuits look like two diodes back to back (see Figure 2.19). Normally the base-emitter diode is conducting (with a forward voltage drop, V_{BE}, of approximately 0.7V) and the base-collector diode is reverse-biased.
3. Each transistor has maximum values of I_C, I_B, and V_{CE} that cannot be exceeded without risk of damaging the device. Power dissipation and other limits specified in the manufacturer's data sheet should also be obeyed.
4. The current flowing from collector to emitter (I_C) is roughly proportional to the current input to the base (I_B), shown in Figure 2.20, and can be calculated with the following formula:

$$I_C = h_{FE} \times I_B$$

or

$$I_C = \beta \times I_B$$

Figure 2.18 NPN (Left) and PNP (Right) Transistor Diagrams

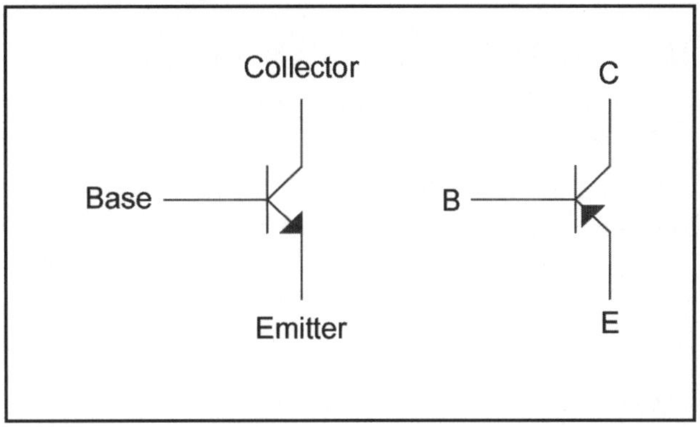

Figure 2.19 Diode Representation of a Transistor, NPN (Left) and PNP (Right)

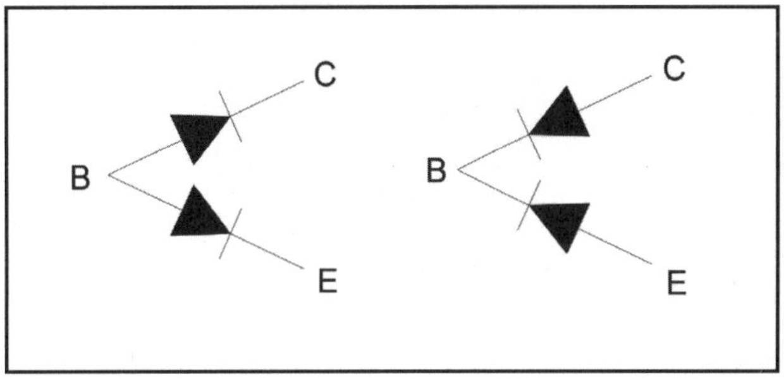

Figure 2.20 NPN Transistor Characteristic Curve

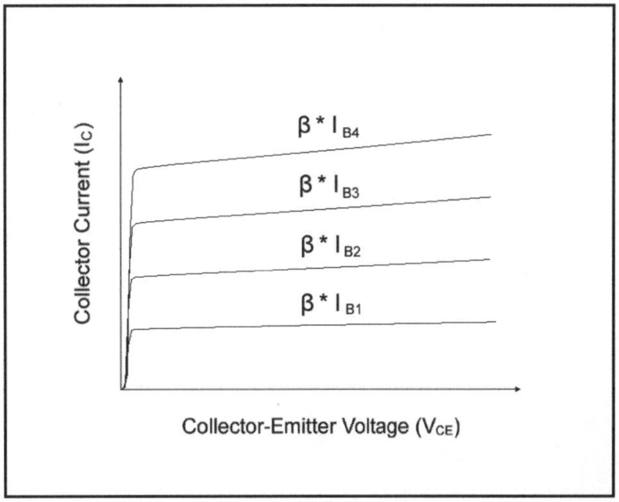

Where h_{FE} (also known as beta, β) is the current gain of the transistor. Typically, β is around 100, though it is not necessarily constant.

Integrated Circuits

Integrated circuits (ICs) combine discrete semiconductor and passive components onto a single microchip of semiconductor material. These may include transistors, diodes, resistors, capacitors, and other circuit components. Unlike discrete components, which usually perform a single function, ICs are capable of performing multiple functions. There are thousands of IC manufacturers, but some familiar ones are Intel, Motorola, and Texas Instruments.

The first generation of commercially available ICs were released by Fairchild and Texas Instruments in 1961 and contained only a few transistors. In comparison, the latest Pentium 4 processor by Intel contains over 175 million transistors in a die area of only 237mm[2] (approximately the size of your thumbnail).

Figure 2.21 Silicon Die Inside an Integrated Circuit

ICs are easy to identify in a circuit by their unique packaging. Typically, the silicon die (containing the microscopic circuitry) is mounted in a plastic or ceramic housing with tiny wires connected to it (see Figure 2.21). The external housing (called a *package*) comes in many mechanical outlines and various pin configurations and spacings.

Figure 2.22 Various IC Package Types

With the constant advances in technology, ICs are shrinking to inconceivable sizes. Figure 2.22 shows a variety of IC packages, including, from left to right, Dual Inline Package (DIP), Narrow DIP, Plastic Leadless Chip Carrier (PLCC), Thin Small Outline Package (TSOP) Type II, TSOP Type I, Small Outline Integrated Circuit (SOIC), Shrink Small Outline Package (SSOP), and Small Outline Transistor (SOT-23).

Ball Grid Array (BGA) is a relatively new package type that locates all the device leads underneath the chip, which reduces the area necessary for the device (see Figure 2.23). However, it is extremely difficult to access the balls of the BGA without completely removing the device, which could be a problem for hardware hacking. BGA devices are becoming more popular due to their small footprint and low failure rates. The testing process (done during product manufacturing) is more expensive than other package types due to the fact that X-rays need to be used to verify that the solder has properly bonded to each of the ball leads.

With Chip-on-Board (COB) packaging, the silicon die of the IC is mounted directly to the PCB and protected by epoxy encapsulation (see Figure 2.24).

Figure 2.23 BGA Packaging

Figure 2.24 COB Packaging

Proper IC positioning is indicated by a dot or square marking (known as a *key*) located on one end of the device (see Figure 2.25). Some devices mark pin 1 with an angled corner (for square package types such as PLCC). On the circuit board, pin 1 is typically denoted by a square pad, whereas the rest of the IC's pads will be circular. Sometimes, a corresponding mark will be silkscreened or otherwise noted on the circuit board. Pin numbers start at the keyed end of the case and progress counter-clockwise around the device, unless noted differently in the specific product data sheet.

Figure 2.25 IC Package Showing Pin Numbers and Key Marking

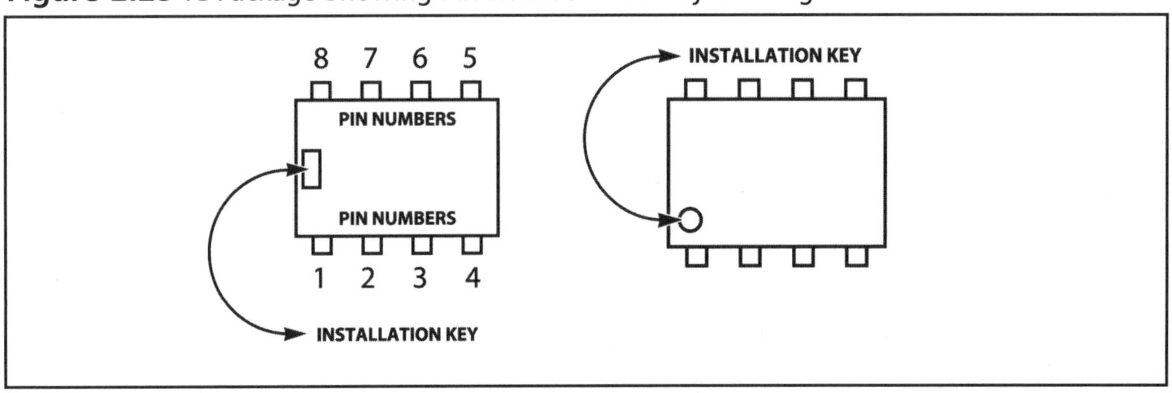

Microprocessors and Embedded Systems

A microprocessor—also known as a microcontroller or CPU (central processing unit), though there are slight technical differences—is essentially a general-purpose computer and is the heart of any embedded system. It is a complete computational engine fabricated on a single integrated circuit. In embedded systems, there is a union of hardware (the underlying circuitry) and software/firmware (code that is executed on the processor). You cannot have one without the other. Just about every electronic device you own can be considered an embedded system.

In November 1971, Intel released the first microprocessor, the Intel 4004. There are now thousands of microprocessors available each with their own benefits and features, including:

- Cost
- Size
- Clock speed
- Data width (for example, 8-, 16-, or 32-bit)
- On-chip peripherals (such as on-chip memory, I/O pins, LCD control, RS232/serial port, USB support, wireless support, analog-to-digital converters, or voltage references)

Common microprocessors include the Intel x86/Pentium-family (used on most personal computers), Motorola 6800- and 68000-families (such as the 68020 or 68030 used in some Macintosh computers or the DragonBall MC68328 used in some Palm PDA devices), ZiLOG Z8, Texas Instruments OMAP, and Microchip PIC.

While we don't cover the specifics of various microprocessors here, we wanted to mention their ubiquity inside hardware products. When you're hardware hacking or reverse engineering a product, chances are that you will encounter a microprocessor of some type. But fear not: Microprocessor data sheets, usually available from the manufacturer, contain instruction sets, register maps, and device-specific details that will give you the inside scoop on how to operate the device. And, once you understand the basic theory of how microprocessors work and the low-level assembly language that they execute, it is fairly trivial to apply that knowledge to a new device or processor family.

Soldering Techniques

Soldering is an art form that requires proper technique in order to be done right. With practice, you will become comfortable and experienced with it. The two key parts of soldering are good heat distribution and cleanliness of the soldering surface and component. In the most basic sense, soldering requires a soldering iron and solder. There are many shapes and sizes of tools to choose from (you can find more details in Chapter 1 "Tools of the Warranty Voiding Trade"). This section uses hands-on examples to demonstrate proper soldering and desoldering techniques.

WARNING: PERSONAL INJURY

Improper handling of the soldering iron can lead to burns or other physical injuries. Wear safety goggles and other protective clothing when working with solder tools. With temperatures hovering around 700 degrees F, the tip of the soldering iron, molten solder, and flux can quickly sear through clothing and skin. Keep all soldering equipment away from flammable materials and objects. Be sure to turn off the iron when it is not in use and store it properly in its stand.

Hands-On Example: Soldering a Resistor to a Circuit Board

This simple example shows the step-by-step process to solder a through-hole component to a printed circuit board (PCB). We use a piece of prototype PCB and a single resistor (see Figure 2.26). Before you install and solder a part, inspect the leads or pins for oxidation. If the metal surface is dull, sand with fine sandpaper until shiny. In addition, clean the oxidation and excess solder from the soldering iron tip to ensure maximum heat transfer.

Figure 2.26 Prototype PCB and Resistor Used in the Example

Bend and insert the component leads into the desired holes on the PCB. Flip the board to the other side. Slightly bend the lead you will be soldering to prevent the component from falling out when the board is turned upside down (see Figure 2.27).

Figure 2.27 Resistor Inserted into PCB

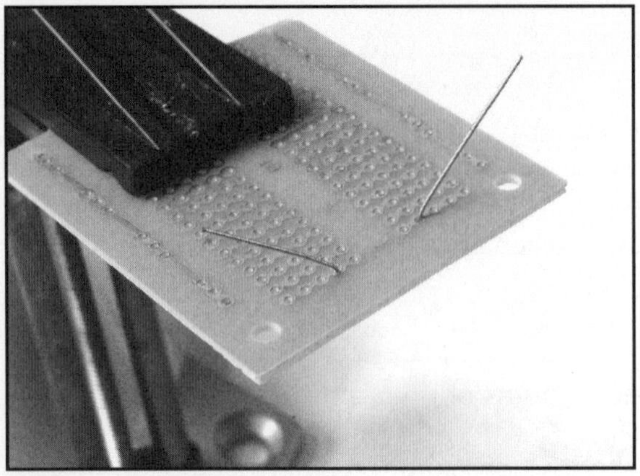

Figure 2.28 Heating the Desired Solder Connection

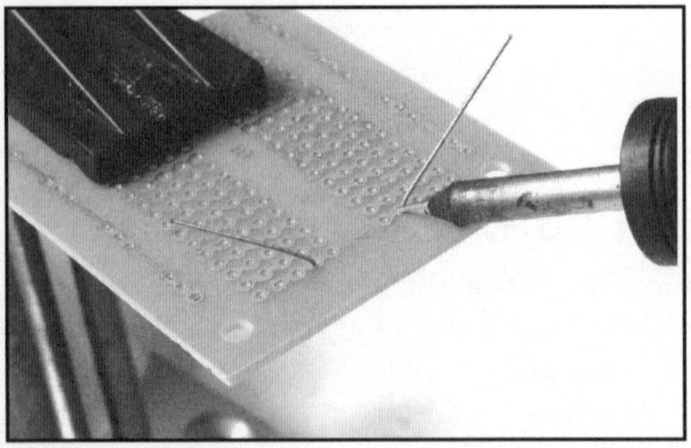

Figure 2.29 Applying Heat and Solder to the Connection

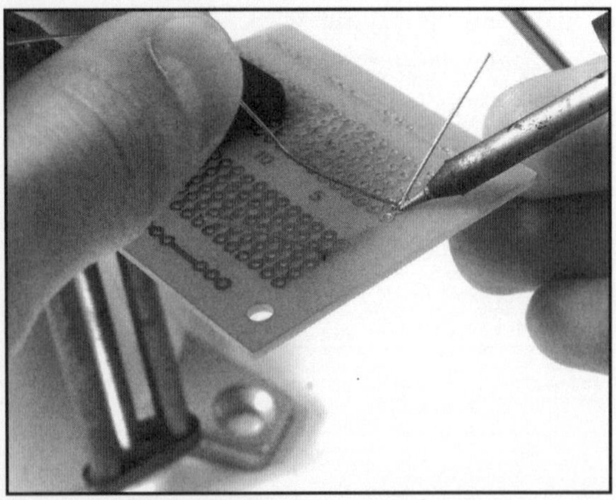

To begin the actual soldering process, allow the tip of your iron to contact both the component lead and the pad on the circuit board for about 1 second before feeding solder to the connection. This will allow the surface to become hot enough for solder to flow smoothly (see Figure 2.28).

Next, apply solder sparingly and hold the iron in place until solder has evenly coated the surface (see Figure 2.29). Ensure that the solder flows all around the two pieces (component lead and PCB pad) that you are fastening together. Do not put solder directly onto the hot iron tip before it has made contact with the lead or pad; doing so can cause a cold solder joint (a common mistake that can prevent your hack from working properly). Soldering is a function of heat, and if the pieces are not heated uniformly, solder may not spread as desired. A cold solder joint will loosen over time and can build up corrosion.

When it appears that the solder has flowed properly, remove the iron from the area and wait a few seconds for the solder to cool and harden. Do not attempt to move the component during this time. The solder joint should appear smooth and shiny, resembling the image in Figure 2.30. If your solder joint has a dull finish, reheat the connection and add more solder if necessary.

Once the solder joint is in place, snip the lead to your desired length (see Figure 2.31). Usually, you will simply cut the remaining portion of the lead that is not part of the actual solder joint (see Figure 2.32). This prevents any risk of short circuits between leftover component leads on the board.

Figure 2.30 Successful Solder Joint

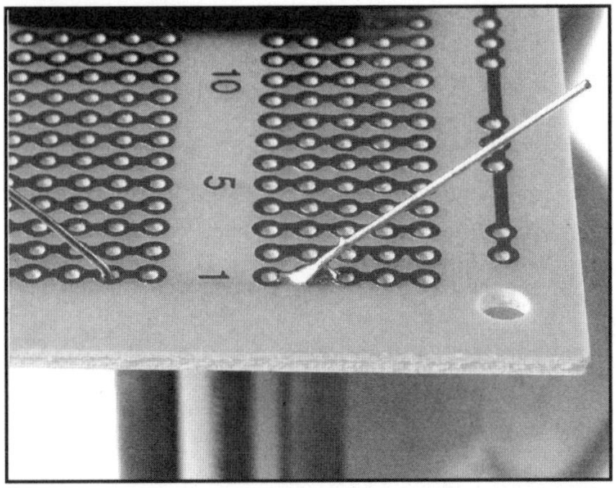

Figure 2.31 Snipping Off the Remaining Component Lead

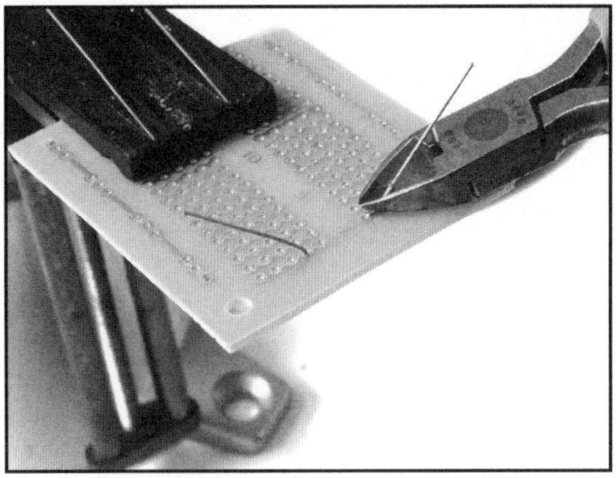

Every so often during any soldering process, use a wet sponge to lightly wipe the excess solder and burned flux from the tip of your soldering iron. This allows the tip to stay clean and heat properly. Proper maintenance of your soldering equipment will also increase its life span.

Figure 2.32 Completed Soldering Example

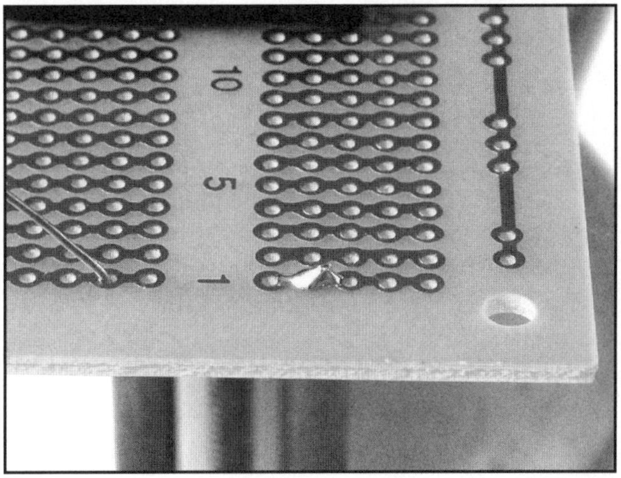

Desoldering Tips

Desoldering, or removing a soldered component from a circuit board, is typically more tricky than soldering, because you can easily damage the device, the circuit board, or surrounding components.

For standard through-hole components, first grasp the component with a pair of needle-nose pliers. Heat the pad beneath the lead you intend to extract and pull gently. The lead should come out. Repeat for the other lead. If solder fills in behind the lead as you extract it, use a spring-loaded solder sucker to remove the excess solder.

For through-hole ICs or multipin parts, use a solder sucker or desoldering braid to remove excess from the hole before attempting to extract the part. You can use a small flat-tip screwdriver or IC extraction tool to help loosen the device from the holes. Be careful to not overheat components, since they can become damaged and may fail during operation. If a component is damaged during extraction, simply replace it with a new part. For surface mount devices (SMDs) with more than a few pins, the easiest method to remove the part is by using the ChipQuik SMD Removal Kit, as shown in the following step-by-step example. Removal of SMD and BGA devices is normally accomplished with special hot-air rework stations. These stations provide a directed hot-air stream used with specific nozzles, depending on the type of device to be removed. The hot air can flow freely around and under the device, allowing the device to be removed with minimal risk of overheating. Rework stations are typically priced beyond the reach of hobbyist hardware hackers, and the ChipQuik kit works quite well as a low-cost alternative.

Hands-On Example: SMD Removal Using ChipQuik

The ChipQuik SMD Removal Kit (www.chipquik.com) allows you to quickly and easily remove surface mount components such as PLCC, SOIC, TSOP, QFP, and discrete packages. The primary component of the kit is a low-melting temperature solder (requiring less than 300 degrees F) that reduces the overall melting temperature of the solder on the SMD pads. Essentially, this enables you to just lift the part right off the PCB.

WARNING: HARDWARE HARM

Please read through this example completely before attempting SMD removal on an actual device. When removing the device, be careful to not scratch or damage any of the surrounding components or pull up any PCB traces. After following the instructions on the package (which consists of simply applying a standard no-clean flux to the SMD pins and then applying a low-melting-point solder), you can easily remove the surface mount part from the board.

Figure 2.33 shows the contents of the basic ChipQuik SMD Removal Kit, from top to bottom: alcohol pads for cleaning the circuit board after device removal, the special low-melting temperature alloy, standard no-clean flux, and application syringe.

Figure 2.33 ChipQuik SMD Removal Kit Contents

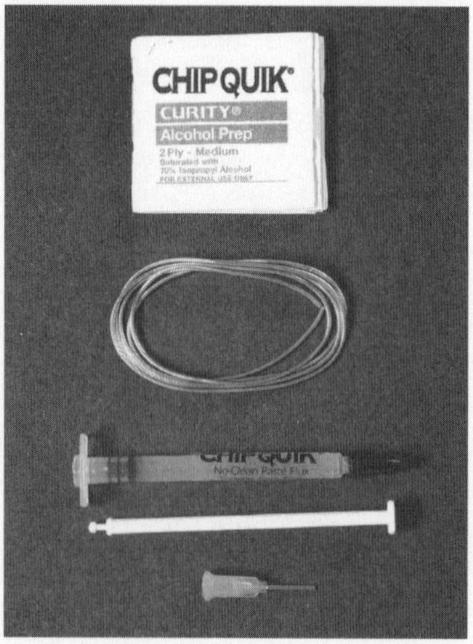

Figure 2.34 Circuit Board Before Part Removal

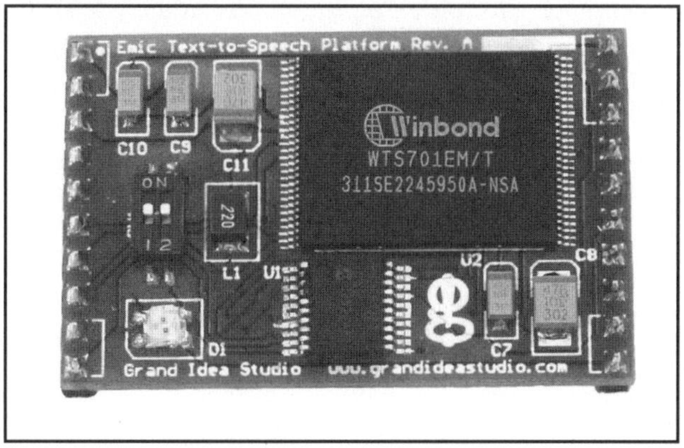

Figure 2.35 Applying Flux to the Leads

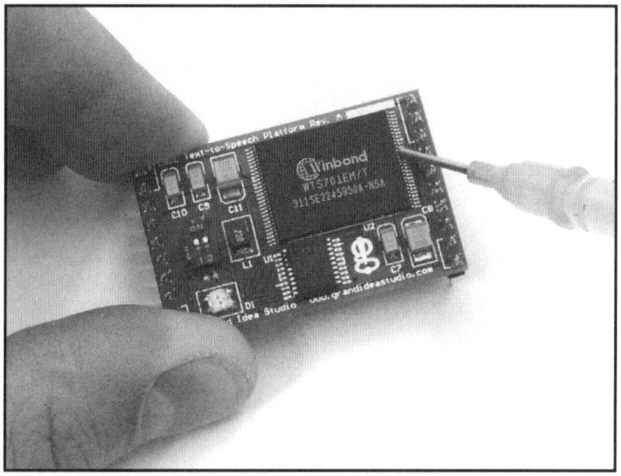

Figure 2.36 Chip with Flux Applied

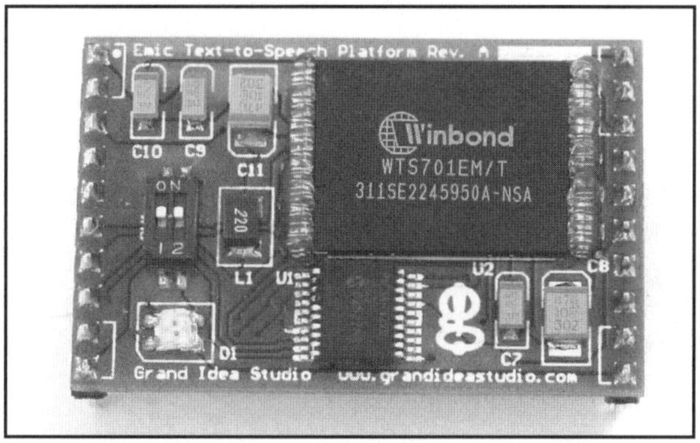

Figure 2.34 shows the circuit board before the SMD part removal. Our target device to remove is the largest device on the board, the Winbond WTS701EM/T 56-pin TSOP IC.

The first step is to assemble the syringe, which contains the no-clean flux. Simply insert the plunger into the syringe and push down to dispense the compound (see Figure 2.35). The flux should be applied evenly across all the pins on the package you will be removing (see Figure 2.36). Flux is a chemical compound used to assist in the soldering or removal of electronic components or other metals. It has three primary functions:

1. Cleans metals surfaces to assist the flow of filler metals (solder) over base metals (device pins)
2. Assists with heat transfer from heat source (soldering iron) to metal surface (device pins)
3. Helps in the removal of surface metal oxides (created by oxygen in the air when the metal reaches high temperatures)

Once the flux is evenly spread over the pins of the target device, the next step is to apply the special ChipQuik alloy to the device (see Figure 2.37). This step is just like soldering: Apply heat to the pins of the device and the alloy at the same time. The alloy has a melting point of approximately 300 degrees F, which is quite low. You should not have to heat the alloy with the soldering iron for very long before it begins to melt. The molten alloy should flow around and under the device pins (see Figure 2.38).

Figure 2.37 Applying Heat and Alloy to the Leads

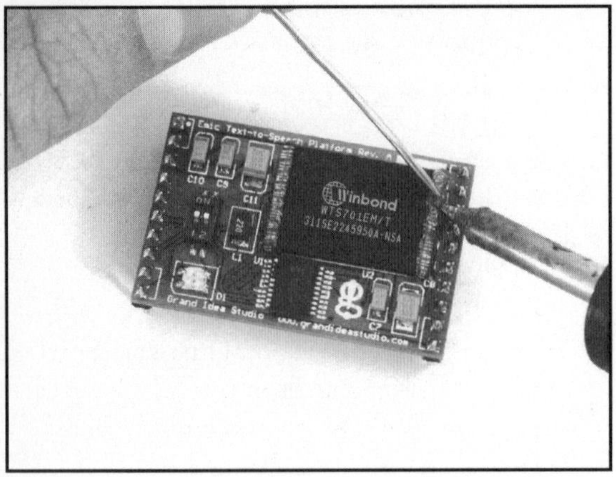

Now that the alloy has been properly applied to all pins of the device, it is time to remove the device from the board. After making sure that the alloy is still molten by reheating all of it with the soldering iron, gently slide the component off the board (see Figure 2.39). You can use a small jeweler's flathead screwdriver to help with the task. If the device is stuck, reheat the alloy and wiggle the part back and forth to help the alloy flow underneath the pads of the device and loosen the connections.

The final step in the desoldering process is to clean the circuit board. This step is important because it will remove any impurities left behind from the ChipQuik process and leave you ready for the next step in your hardware hack.

First, use the soldering iron to remove any stray alloy left on the device pads or anywhere else on the circuit board. Next, apply a thin, even layer of flux to all of the pads that the device was just soldered to. Use the included alcohol swab or a flux remover spray to remove the flux and clean the area (see Figure 2.40).

Starting at one end of the device, simply heat and apply the alloy. Repeat for the other side(s) of the device. The flux will help with ensuring a nice flow of the alloy onto the device pins. Ensure that the alloy has come in contact with every single pin by gently moving the soldering iron around the edges of the device. Avoid touching nearby components on the PCB with the soldering iron.

Figure 2.38 Chip with Alloy Applied

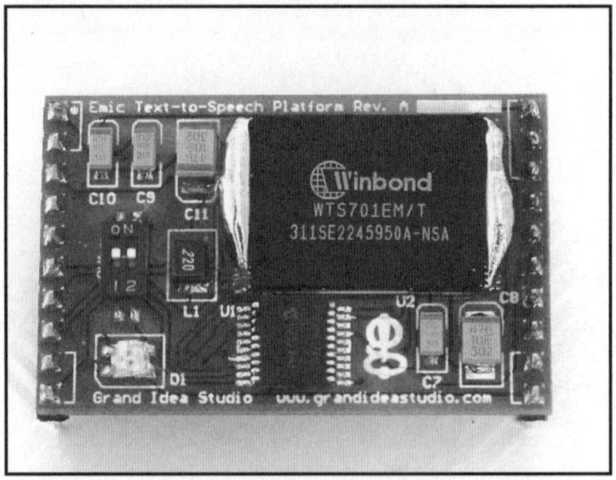

Figure 2.39 Removing the Device from the Board

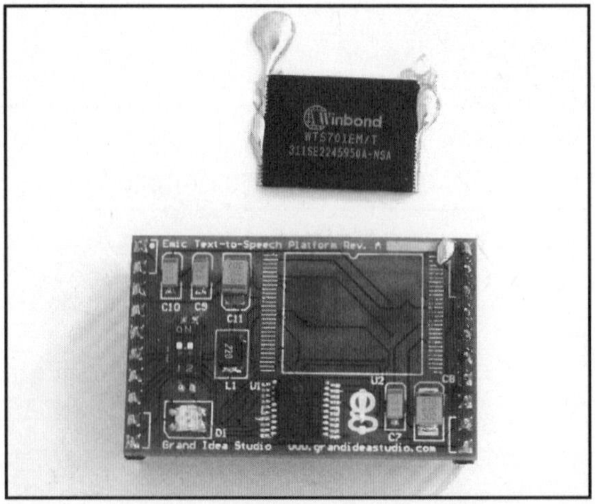

Figure 2.40 Using Flux and Alcohol Swab to Clean Area

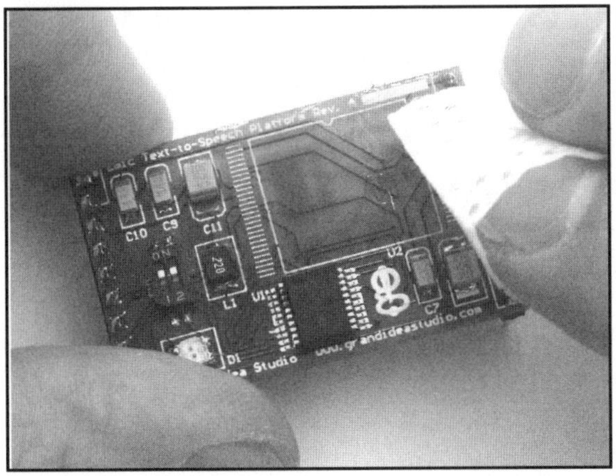

Figure 2.41 Circuit Board with Part Successfully Removed

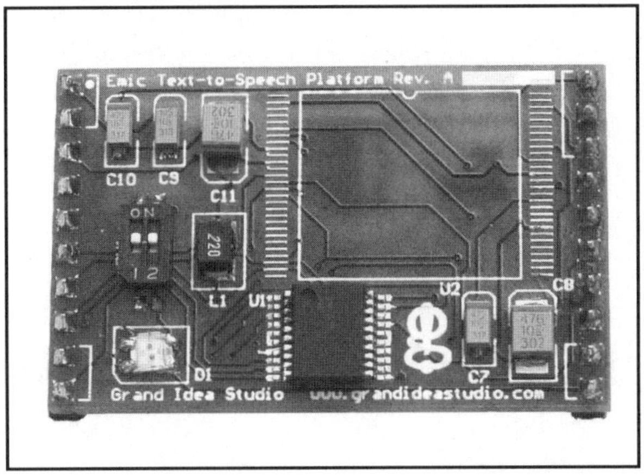

The desoldering process is now complete. The surface mount device has been removed and the circuit board cleaned (see Figure 2.41). If you intend to reuse the device you just removed, use the soldering iron to remove any stray alloy or solder left over on and in between the pins and ensure there are no solder bridges between pins. If you do not want to reuse the device, simply throw it away.

Common Engineering Mistakes

During engineering design and debugging, you should remember the important maxim K.I.S.S.—or Keep It Simple, Stupid—at all times. It can be frustrating to troubleshoot a problem for hours or days on end and then discover the cause was a simple oversight. The most common engineering mistakes for hardware hacking are listed here. Although there are hundreds of other simple mistakes that can cause an engineer to quickly lose his or her hair, this list should get you started:

- **Faulty solder connections** After soldering, inspect the connections for cold solder joints and solder bridges. Cold solder joints happen when you don't fully heat the connection or when metallic corrosion and oxide contaminate a component lead or pad. Cold solder joints are the most common mistake for amateur and hobbyist electronics builders. Solder bridges form when a trail of excess solder shorts pads or tracks together (see the "Soldering Techniques" section in this chapter).
- **Installing the wrong part** Verify the part type and value before you insert and solder the component to the circuit board. Although many devices appear to look similar (e.g., a 1K and a 10K resistor look almost the same except for the color of one band), they have different operating characteristics and may act very differently in an electronic circuit. Surface mount components are typically harder to distinguish from one another. Double check to ensure that each part is installed properly. Keep in mind that the only way to properly test a component's value is to remove it from the board and then test it.

- **Installing parts backward** ICs have a notch or dot at one end indicating the correct direction of insertion. Electrolytic capacitors have a marking to denote the negative lead (on polarized surface mount capacitors, the positive lead has the marking). Through-hole capacitors also have a shorter-length negative lead than the positive lead. Transistors have a flat side or emitter tab to help you identify the correct mounting position and are often marked to identify each pin. Diodes have a banded end indicating the cathode side of the device.
- **Verify power** Ensure that the system is properly receiving the desired voltages from the power supply. If the device uses batteries, check to make sure that they have a full charge and are installed properly. If your device isn't receiving power, chances are it won't work.

Web Links and Other Resources

We end this chapter by citing material that will provide you with more information on electrical engineering.

General Electrical Engineering Books

- Radio Shack offers a wide variety of electronic hobby and "how to" books, including an Engineer's Notebook series of books that provide an introduction to formulas, tables, basic circuits, schematic symbols, integrated circuits, and optoelectronics (light-emitting diodes and light sensors). Other books cover topics on measurement tools, amateur radio, and computer projects.
- *Nuts & Volts* (www.nutsvolts.com) and *Circuit Cellar* (www.circuitcellar.com) magazines are geared toward both electronics hobbyists and professionals. Both are produced monthly and contain articles, tutorials, and advertisements for all facets of electronics and engineering.
- Horowitz and Hill, *The Art of Electronics*, Cambridge University Press, 1989, ISBN 0-52-137095-7. Essential reading for basic electronics theory. It is often used as a course textbook in university programs.
- C. R. Robertson, *Fundamental Electrical & Electronic Principles*, Newnes, 2001, ISBN 0-75-065145-8. Covers the essential principles that form the foundations for electrical and electronic engineering courses.
- M. M. Mano, *Digital Logic and Computer Design,* Prentice-Hall, 1979, ISBN 0-13-214510-3. Digital logic design techniques, binary systems, Boolean algebra and logic gates, simplification of Boolean functions, and digital computer system design methods.
- K. R. Fowler, *Electronic Instrument Design*, Oxford University Press, 1996, ISBN 0-19-508371-7. Provides a complete view of the product development life cycle. Offers practical design solutions, engineering trade-offs, and numerous case studies.

Electrical Engineering Web Sites

- **ePanorama.net: www.epanorama.net** A clearing house of electronics information found on the Web. The content and links are frequently updated. Copious amounts of information for electronics professionals, students, and hobbyists.
- **The EE Compendium, The Home of Electronic Engineering and Embedded Systems Programming: http://ee.cleversoul.com** Contains useful information for professional electronics engineers, students, and hobbyists. Features many papers, tutorials, projects, book recommendations, and more.
- **Discover Circuits: www.discovercircuits.com** A resource for engineers, hobbyists, inventors, and consultants, Discover Circuits is a collection of over 7,000 electronic circuits and schematics cross-references into more than 500 categories for finding quick solutions to electronic design problems.
- **WebEE, The Electrical Engineering Homepage: www.web-ee.com** Large reference site of schematics, tutorials, component information, forums, and links.
- **Electro Tech Online: www.electro-tech-online.com** A community of free electronic forums. Topics include general electronics, project design, microprocessors, robotics, and theory.
- **University of Washington EE Circuits Archive: www.ee.washington.edu/circuit_archive** A large of collection of circuits, data sheets, and electronic-related software.

Data Sheets and Component Information

When reverse engineering a product for hardware hacking purposes, identifying components and device functionality is typically an important step. Understanding what the components do may provide detail of a particular area that could be hacked. Nearly all vendors post their component data sheets on the Web for public access, so simple searches will yield a decent amount of information. The following resources will also help you if the vendors don't:

- **Data Sheet Locator: www.datasheetlocator.com** A free electronic engineering tool that enables you to locate product data sheets from hundreds of electronic component manufacturers worldwide.
- **IC Master: www.icmaster.com** The industry's leading source of integrated circuit information, offering product specifications, complete contact information, and Web site links.
- **Integrated Circuit Identification (IC-ID): www.elektronikforum.de/ic-id** Lists of manufacturer logos, names, and datecode information to help identifying unknown integrated circuits.

- **PartMiner: www.freetradezone.com** Excellent resource for finding technical information and product availability and for purchasing electronic components.

Major Electronic Component and Parts Distributors

- Digi-Key, 1-800-344-4539, www.digikey.com
- Mouser Electronics, 1-800-346-6873, www.mouser.com
- Newark Electronics, 1-800-263-9275, www.newark.com
- Jameco, 1-800-831-4242, www.jameco.com

Obsolete and Hard-to-Find Component Distributors

When trying to locate obscure, hard-to-find materials and components, don't give up easily. Sometimes it will take hours of phone calls and Web searching to find exactly what you need. Many companies that offer component location services have a minimum order (upward of $100 or $250), which can easily turn a hobbyist project into one collecting dust on a shelf. Some parts-hunting tips:

- Go to the manufacturer Web site and look for any distributors or sales representatives. For larger organizations, you probably won't be able to buy directly from the manufacturer. Call your local distributor or representative to see if they have access to stock. They will often sample at small quantities or have a few-piece minimum order.
- Be creative with Google searches. Try the base part name, manufacturer, and combinations thereof.
- Look for cross-reference databases or second-source manufacturers. Many chips have compatible parts that can be used directly in place.

The following companies specialize in locating obsolete and hard-to-find components. Their service is typically not inexpensive, but as a last resort to find the exact device you need, these folks will most likely find one for you somewhere in the world:

- USBid, www.usbid.com
- Graveyard Electronics, 1-800-833-6276, www.graveyardelectronics.com
- Impact Components, 1-800-424-6854, www.impactcomponents.com
- Online Technology Exchange, 1-800-606-8459, www.onlinetechx.com

Chapter 3

Operating Systems Overview

Topics in this Chapter:

- OS Basics
- Drivers
- Linux/UNIX
- VxWorks
- Windows CE

Introduction

A computer without any operating software is just an expensive pile of metal, plastic, and silicon. Physically, a computer contains processors, memory, disks, and input/output devices such as keyboards, monitors, and drives. The operating system (OS) is the software or firmware that controls all of these components. When you are writing a program, you don't usually know the physical layout of every computer your program will be run on. If you did know, you certainly wouldn't want to waste your time telling your program exactly how to store data on a hard disk. The OS's job is to take care of that low-level hardware access information for you. The OS's other job is to monitor resource allocation. Your computer might be running two programs, such as a Web browser and an e-mail program, at the same time. They can't both use the physical network interface simultaneously. The OS assigns physical resources to each application so the application designers don't have to worry about such things.

Need to Know.... Understanding Layering

This description of a computer's physical versus software layers is a simplification. Most computers are likely to have multiple layers of increasing abstraction in order to work:

- Physical devices (processor, disks, etc.)
- Microprogramming interpreter for the machine language
- Machine language
- Operating system
- System programs
- Application programs

If you do a lot of operating system programming, you'll want to learn more about how these layers interact.

OS Basics

Many different types of operating systems exist, ranging from Microsoft Windows, Mac OS, and Linux for desktop PCs, to Symbian OS, Palm OS, Windows CE, and VxWorks for embedded systems and mobile devices. This chapter briefly presents the high-level concepts of operating systems. Specific features will vary depending on which OS you are interested in. In this section, we introduce you to some of the fundamental concepts of operating systems:

- Memory
- File systems
- Input and output
- Processes
- System calls
- The shell

Need to Know… Memory or Disk?

It's easy to get confused between the terms *memory* (or *RAM*) and *disk* (or *hard drive*). We'll get into details in this chapter, but for now, just be aware that *memory* is temporary storage that goes away when the computer is turned off, and *disk* is permanent storage that exists even when the computer has no power.

Memory

In a computer system, memory, or *random access memory* (*RAM*), is used to hold temporary information. It's very fast, but it's also volatile—it goes away when you turn off the computer or when battery power is removed. Whatever a program is doing at any given moment needs to be tracked in memory. Managing memory is one of the OS's most important jobs.

Physical Memory

Physical memory is a type of hardware that the computer can retrieve information from very quickly. Information stored at any address on the hardware can be directly accessed with an address that refers to a specific location on the hardware. Because this direct access allows information to be retrieved from any random point in memory, this sort of memory is known as *random access memory* (RAM).

As Figure 3.1 illustrates, a program can request the information that is stored in physical memory at any location. Here the program requests the data stored in physical memory at the location addressed *0K*. The information in that memory location—in this illustration, the letter *A*—is returned to the program.

Figure 3.1 Memory Management: Direct Access to Physical Memory

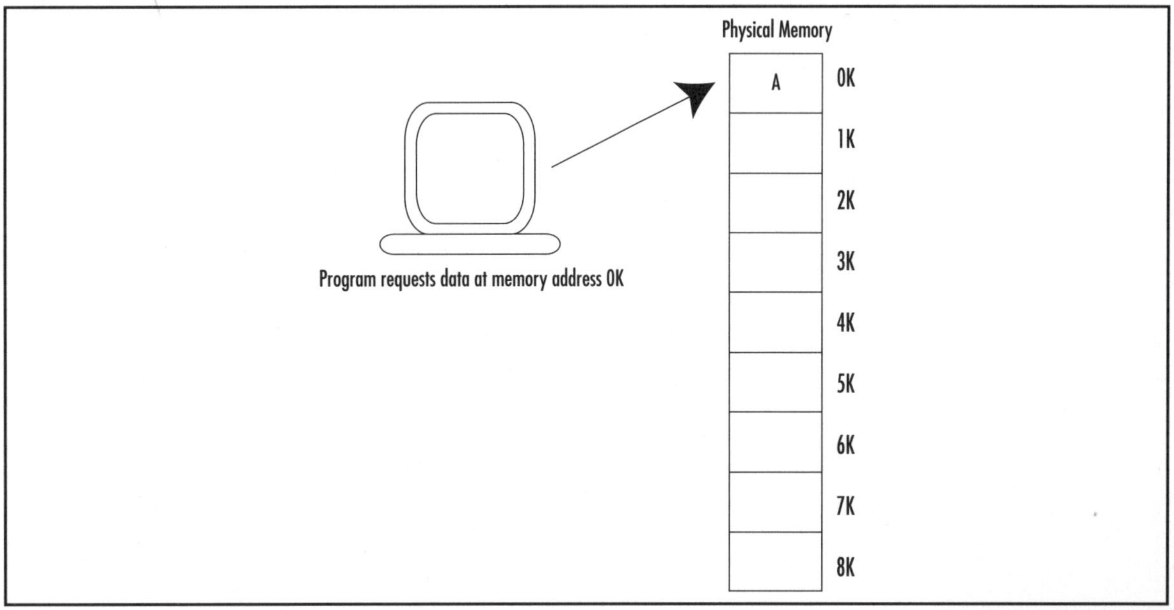

NEED TO KNOW… ALPHABET SOUP

The basic unit of measurement computers use is a *bit*. A bit represents a 0 or a 1, and you can think of it as a kind of on/off switch. When the switch is on and electricity is running, that's a 1. When the switch is off and the electricity stops flowing, that's a 0. In a nutshell, all a computer does is manage these pulses of electrical energy, these ones and zeros.

We don't usually talk in bits. The smallest reasonable size that we deal with on a computer is a *byte*. A byte is 8 bits, and as you can see, that is still pretty small. It takes about a byte to store a single character such as, say, this one: A. Or this one: B. Writing "hack" requires four bytes, or 32 bits.

- *K*, *kB*, and *KB* are abbreviations for *kilobyte*, which means is 1,024 bytes.
- *M* and *MB* are abbreviations for *megabyte*, which is 1,024KB or 1,048,576 bytes.
- *G* and *GB* are abbreviations for *gigabyte*, which is 1,024MB or 1,073,741,824 bytes.

You can find more details about this terminology in Chapter 2, "Electrical Engineering Basics."

The OS manages memory in the appropriately named *memory manager*. The memory manager keeps track of what memory is being used, allocates unused memory to processes that request it, and takes care of which memory is stored in your physical memory and which is temporarily stashed on your hard drive.

Wait, why are we storing memory on the hard drive? See, even though memory gets cheaper all the time, disks get cheaper all the time, too. And you're always going to have more disk space than you have memory, so why not take advantage of the cheaper resource? Moreover, some computers have hardware limitations on the amount of memory that can be made available to a single program, but a programmer might want to use more memory than that limit allows. This is where virtual memory comes in.

Virtual Memory

Virtual memory maps logical memory addresses to physical memory addresses. The hard disk can be used as if it were cheap—and slow—memory. The memory manager takes care of remembering which information lives on the physical memory and which information is stored on the hard disk. A program doesn't have to worry about where the memory is stored, because that information is hidden from it. The memory manager creates artificial memory addresses, presents them to the program, and takes care of the translation itself.

Figure 3.2 illustrates this translation. The program on the computer requests the data stored at the location addressed *0K*. The memory manager looks at its memory map and sees that the virtual address *0K* corresponds to the physical address *5K*. The memory manager retrieves the data from physical memory—in Figure 3.2, the letter *A*—and returns it to the calling program. The program never learns that the information was actually stored in a different location in physical memory, because the memory manager takes care of the translation behind the scenes.

Figuring out which sections of code can easily be parceled out to RAM rather than to the hard disk can be a job either for the OS designer or for the conscientious application designer who wants her program to run very quickly.

Figure 3.2 Memory Management: Virtual Memory

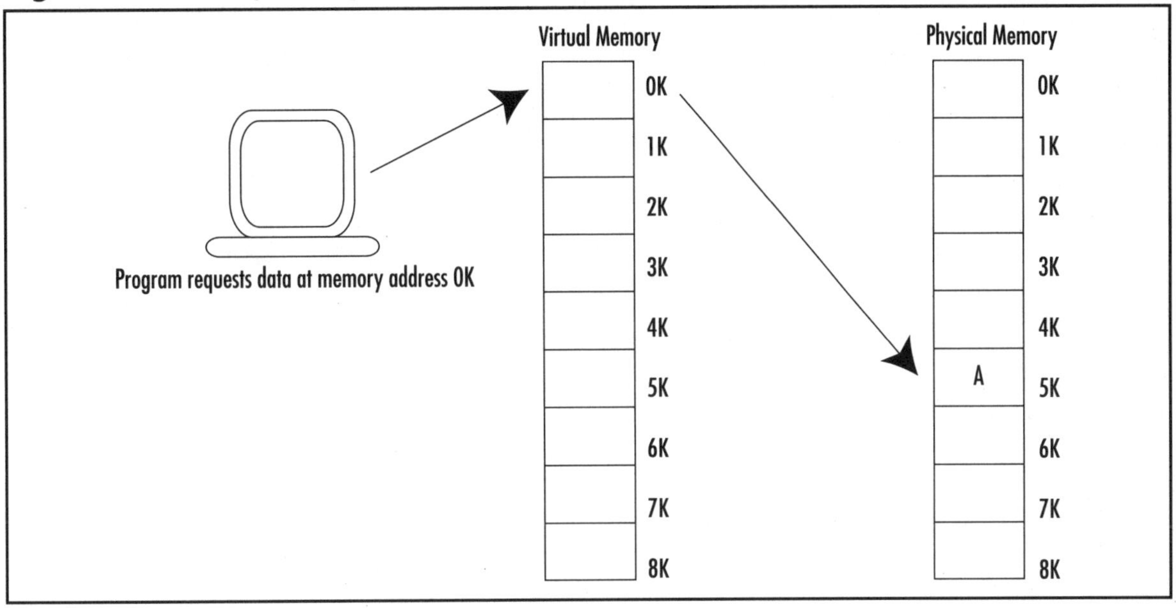

Need to Know...A Note on Terminology

Strictly speaking, you can have a virtual memory system without using your hard disk for memory at all. All a virtual memory system does is map real, physical memory addresses to artificial memory addresses that are presented to the application.

As you can see, the term virtual memory refers to all memory that is accessed through the virtual memory manager, whether it is RAM, hard disk, or other storage medium. And both RAM and the hard disk are forms of physical memory. In general usage, though, you'll often see the term "physical memory" used to refer to RAM, and virtual memory used to refer to that portion of your memory that is being stored on your hard disk.

File Systems

Let's face it, it doesn't matter how good your computer is if there isn't a place to store files and data. The file system provides a structure to how data is stored on a storage medium, like a hard drive or DVD.

Your storage needs to be long-term. We don't need to get into the electrical engineering of how long-term information is physically stored, but let's think about the logical structure for moment. There's a lot of bytes of information on your hard disk. If you have to go rifling through all those bytes every time you need to find your Web browser, you're going to spend a lot of the day looking for programs and files. So your storage needs to not only last but to be *accessible*. It also needs to be accessible to multiple programs at once. Even though your average home user doesn't need concurrent access to very large numbers of files, he's still playing music files that he can also view in a folder listing, or he's editing the alarms on his PDA while the clock program keeps track of which alarms are coming up.

The most important thing from the user's perspective is what the files are named and whether or not they can be accessed. Filenames and file paths are just logical ways of looking at a collection of bytes that might be spread out all over a physical disk. Consider the following example for the Windows OS: When you tell your computer "I'd like the file C:\My Documents\Invitations\garden-party.doc" (see Figure 3.3), it doesn't have some special drawer to find that information in. Instead, your computer might have an index to the top level of the C: drive. It will look in that file to figure out where to find information about the directory My Documents. This will send it to some other portion of the disk, where it might find another index file that has information about all files in that directory. The computer will look in this index file, which represents the My Documents directory, and find a pointer to an index file that represents the Invitations directory. At last, in the index file of the Invitations directory, the computer will find a pointer to the location of the file named garden-party.doc. This is a pretty simplified view of the process, but it covers the basics. Depending on the OS or device you are using, there are different systems available, such as FAT32 or NTFS for Windows, HFS+ for Macintosh, ext2 for Linux, or JFFS for Flash memory devices in embedded systems. The way data is accessed and handled will vary between different operating systems.

The file system also keeps track of whether or not you have permission to read, write, or execute the file in question. These are the *attributes* of the file. The file system is what lets you read, write, create, and delete files. If areas of the physical disk are bad and no longer able to store data, the file system can keep track of that information so the computer doesn't attempt to write to those blocks of the disk (Some disks can also keep track of that information themselves, using on-board firmware.)

Figure 3.3 A Hierarchical File System Example

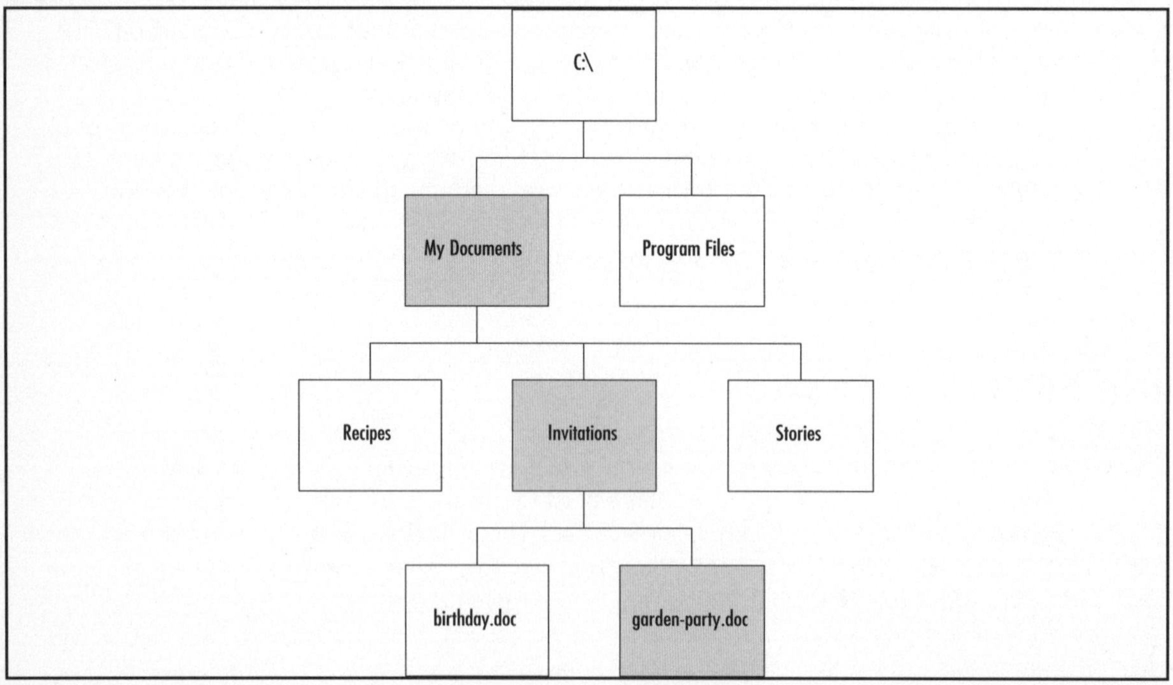

Cache

Remember how we mentioned that disks are much slower to access than memory? Operating system designers have different ways to speed up access to hard disks. *Cache* can be thought of as the opposite of virtual memory. Where the virtual memory manager is used to store information that logically belongs in memory on the physical hard disks, cache is used to store information that logically belongs on the disk in—you guessed it—memory.

Reading from memory and writing to memory are much faster than reading from disk and writing to disk, so for frequent read/write operations, using a cache will make the computer much faster. Of course, information in memory is dynamic and gets lost in the event of a power failure, unlike information in a hard disk. Operating system designers have come up with various strategies to prevent data loss from the cache in the event of a computer crash. The balance is always between efficiency and safety. The most efficient method is to synchronize data between the cache and hard disks on a regular basis—say, every 30 seconds. Less efficient, but far less likely to lose data in the event of a crash, is a *write-through cache*, which writes data to the disk every time some predetermined size of data, maybe 1KB, is written to the cache.

Input/Output

Inputs and outputs are how we communicate with our computers. We use keyboards, mice, trackballs, CD-ROMs, and network connections to put information into the computer. We use monitors, speakers, discs, and network connections to get information out. A computer without input/output capabilities could be the most powerful system in the world and still be useless.

An OS is responsible for controlling all of these physical input and output devices. It handles the low-level interaction with the hardware and abstracts from the user, so they don't have to be concerned about it. It needs to be able to send commands to each of the devices. The OS needs to be able to handle when things go wrong and "listen" to interrupt messages from the various hardware devices.

Processes

Your computer at home can play music while you browse the Web and have a word processor open in the background with a term paper you have to finish. Your TiVo can play back a television program and record one at the same time. Even your PDA can display your address book while keeping track of the alarm clock you have set. All modern computers can do multiple things simultaneously.

Once you have multiple processes, you need a way to manage them, which is another task for the operating system. Multiple processes are all competing for the same system resources. Your Web browser needs your hard disk (to check your bookmarks and to record cache information), your memory (to save information about the parts of Windows that aren't currently visible on your screen), and your sound card (when you get to that annoying Web page that plays a little tune when you load it). But your music program also needs your hard disk (where your music files are stored), your memory (where it has saved the play list you requested), and your sound card (to play the music)! How do these two programs decide which program gets the resource, if they request access to the hard disk at the same time?

For example, if your TiVo is going to record *Survivor* at 8:00 P.M., it can't be busy thinking about how to play back an old episode of *The Simpsons* at the same time. You'll get very cranky if you tell your TiVo to play back that episode where Homer sells his soul for a doughnut, and it tells you "Please be patient. I'm trying to record *Survivor*." How does your TiVo manage to start recording *Survivor* on time without making you notice any unacceptable delays? Elegant solutions to these problems are an essential part of an operating system.

NEED TO KNOW... DINING PHILOSOPHERS

If you decide to devote further study to OS concepts, be sure to check out the *dining philosophers problem*. Posed by computer scientist Edsger W. Dijkstra in 1965, the dining philosophers problem is one of the classic resource allocation problems of the field, dealing with deadlocks and the problems systems can get into if multiple processes are waiting for each other to finish. How dry can a topic be if one of its classic problems involves five philosophers eating spaghetti around a circular table, without enough forks to go around? One of the goals of any operating system designer is to make sure that none of the philosophers starves.

System Calls

When a developer writes an application, she needs to communicate with the operating system to access files and other resources. She does this by using *system calls*—library functions that other programs can run to give them access to OS functionality, such as file creation. As a general rule, developers writing in high-level languages often won't directly use system calls. Instead, they'll use some higher-level library function, and the high-level function will take care of making the low-level system call, which in turn takes care of issuing instructions to the operating system.

Shells, User Interfaces, and GUIs

All of these memory managers, system calls, and input/output device drivers don't make up the thing on your screen you actually type and mouse at. That's the *shell*, the *command-line interface* (*CLI*), the *user interface* (*UI*), or the *graphical user interface* (*GUI*).

NEED TO KNOW... A NOTE ON TERMINOLOGY

- A *GUI* is always graphical. Microsoft Windows, MacOS X, and X Windows are examples of GUIs.
- A *CLI is* a screen in which you type commands without windows or menus (strictly speaking, anyway, although menu-based programs can be written for text-only terminals). MS-DOS and the UNIX command line are examples of CLIs.
- A *shell* is usually a CLI, though some people use *shell* synonymously with *UI*, to mean any generic user interface.
- A *UI* is either textual or graphical; it's a generic term for any type of user interface.

The UI is the layer between you and the rest of the OS. When you are clicking on an icon in Windows, using the Dock on a MacOS X system, or typing a command on a UNIX system, you're using the UI.

Device Drivers

What would we do if there weren't *device drivers*? Say you wanted a program to read a file from a hard disk. Without a device driver, you would need to know how many sectors and cylinders the disk had, what kind of motor it used, what commands were used to control the read/write arm, and all sorts of detailed low-level mechanicsof the hardware.

Figure 3.4 illustrates a very simplified program talking to devices without the use of device drivers. Any program that operates without device drivers needs to be able to communicate directly with every piece of hardware that we might use while running the program. It doesn't just need to know how to move a disk arm to a cylinder—it needs to know how to move the disk arm on every possible model of hard drive to a cylinder. (This description is something of an oversimplification: Some of the work is done by the hard disk's on-board firmware. But, there's still an enormous amount that the OS needs to know before it can talk to a disk.)

Figure 3.4 A Program Interacting Directly With Diverse Devices

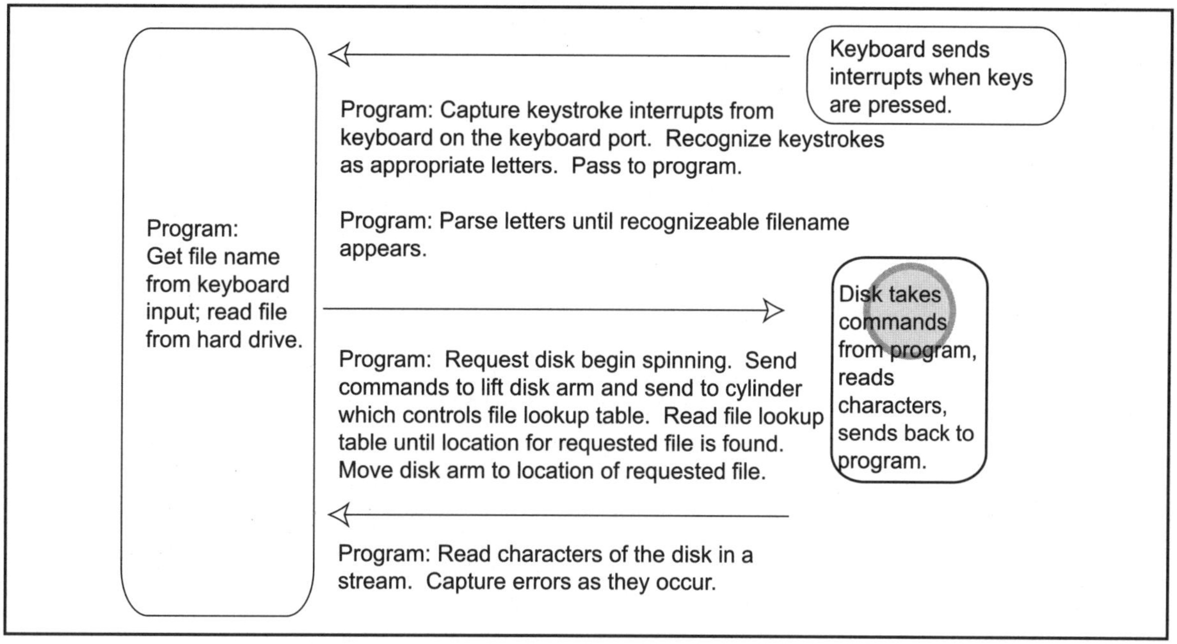

Warning: Hardware Harm

People who know the intricate details and design of the hardware generally write the device drivers. Usually the hardware or OS manufacturer will provide the necessary device drivers, but sometimes you'll need to write your own. For example, a device driver might be unavailable for your hardware, or the available device driver might be unnecessarily conservative or restrictive. If you aren't sure of the physical limitations of the device—maximum safe clock speed of your processor, for example, or maximum safe refresh rate of your monitor—you can do irreparable harm to your equipment. When writing your own device driver, be sure you know the physical limitations of the hardware! Exciting as the smell of melted processor can be (and yes, this really does happen), it's probably not what you want to wake up to.

The job of the device driver is to know all the information about the hardware for you. All your application needs to do is tell the device driver, "Read this information from this disk." The device driver translates your request into a detailed sequence of commands that instruct the physical disk how to find and read your information, as we can see in Figure 3.5.

Figure 3.5 A Program Interacting With Device Drivers Between It and the Hardware

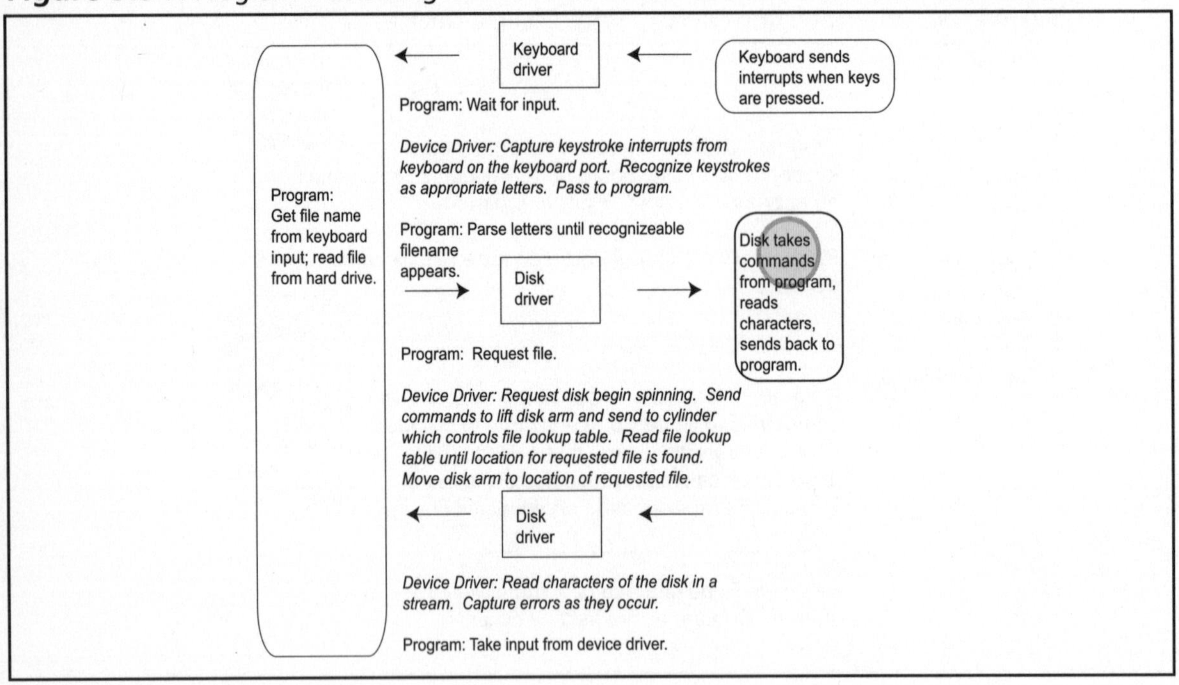

Anything hardware-specific that the OS needs to know goes into the device drivers. A simple device driver might be able to handle an entire class of devices—all serial mice, for example. A more complex and device-specific device driver might be needed to make best use of some piece of hardware's special features, such as a mouse with a scroll wheel.

Block and Character Devices

There are two main kinds of input/output devices: character devices and block devices. A *character device* doesn't have fixed-size *blocks* (chunks of data that the device sends to be processed one at a time) and can only be accessed in order: the first piece of data, followed by the second, followed by the third, and so on. Character devices deal with streams of characters. A network connection is a character device, as is a keyboard connection. A roll of sticky tape can be thought of as a sort of character device. You can take any amount of sticky tape you want, but you can't get to the tape in the middle until you've dealt with the tape at the beginning of the roll (see Figure 3.6).

Figure 3.6 Sticky Tape Seen as a Character Device

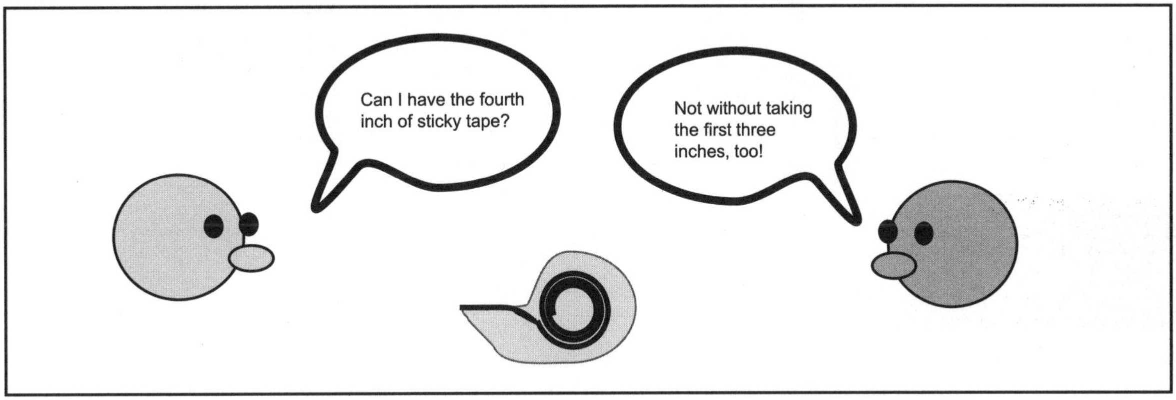

Just like a roll of sticky tape, the tape drive illustrated in Figure 3.7 works as a character device, giving you each unit of data in the order it appears on the tape, without letting you skip directly to the part you want.

Figure 3.7 A Tape Drive as a Character Device

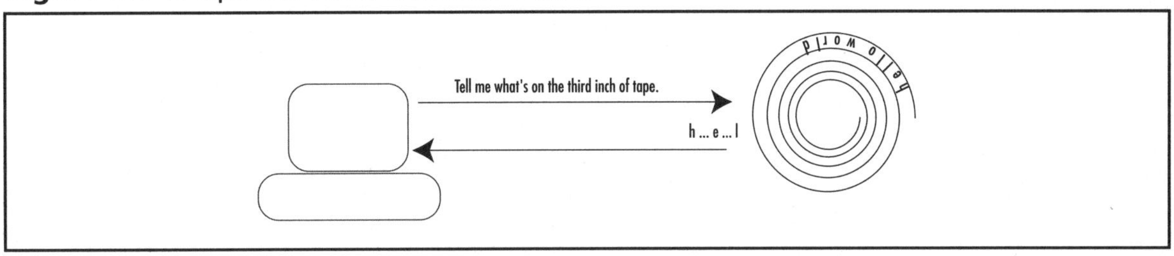

Block devices, such as hard drives and optical media (DVDs and CD-ROMs), store information in addressable blocks of a fixed size. Any block on a block device can be accessed directly; the blocks don't need to be accessed in order, as they do with a character device. A bookshelf, illustrated in Figure 3.8, can be thought of as a block device. Each book on a bookshelf is a block of information, and you can pick up any book directly without going through any other book.

Figure 3.8 A Bookshelf as Block Device

A standard hard drive is one of the most common block devices. In Figure 3.9, a program requests the data that is stored on sector 2 of a hard drive and receives that data directly, without having to first read sector 1.

Figure 3.9 A Block Device With Direct Access to any Block

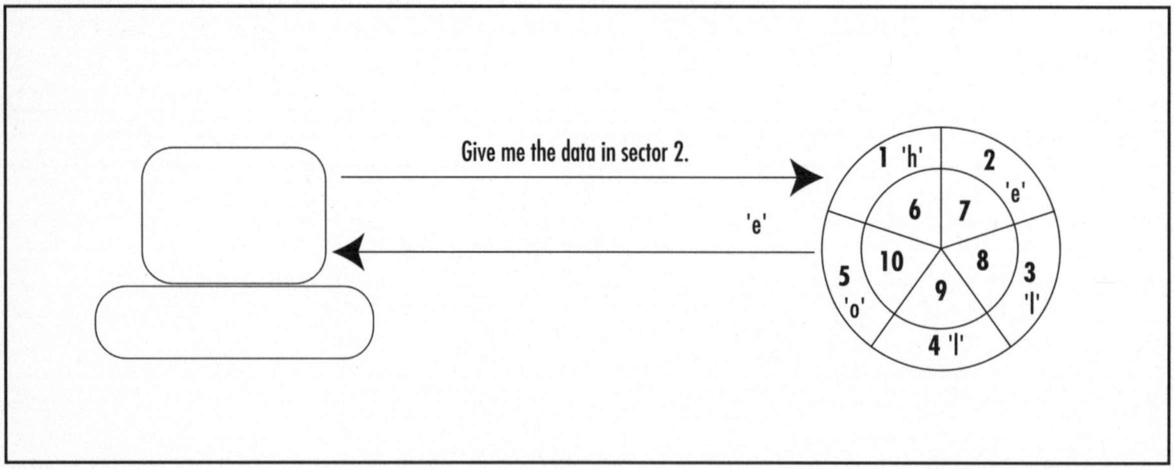

NOTE

If you are in interested in more detailed information on the topic of device drivers, take a look at the following books:

- *Linux Device Drivers*, by Alessandro Rubini and Jonathan Corbet (O'Reilly, 2001). Available online at www.xml.com/ldd/chapter/book/.
- *Getting Started with Windows Drivers*. Available online at http://msdn.microsoft.com/library/en-us/gstart/hh/gstart/z_gstart_hdr_5pwn.asp.

Properties of Embedded Operating Systems

In its most simple form, *embedded system* is a special-purpose computer built into a special device. Embedded systems are often designed to run on specialized hardware such as cellular phones, PDAs, and *set-top boxes* (which connect to your television, such as TiVos or computer game systems). Embedded systems have special constraints. Since they are usually included in the category of consumer electronics (although they run the entire spectrum of use—embedded systems are also used in industrial robots and on space missions), embedded systems need to be able to run on cheap, mass-produced hardware often with limited power. Therefore, they must be:

- Inexpensive
- Small (to run on cheap hardware)
- Conservative in power use

A *real-time operating system* (*RTOS*) needs to run in a predictable and deterministic fashion, no matter what is running on the system at any given time. An RTOS is likely to have the following characteristics:

- It will be small, using very little memory (usually a limited resource on embedded systems.)
- Most processes will be preemptable by hardware events of a higher priority.
- The system should have predictable and deterministic response rates for any given operation.

This isn't to say it should be fast—the extra load necessary to keep all events controlled and to give priority where it is needed might make the system relatively slow. But it will be predictable, which is essential. Think about the computer that controls the antilock brakes in your car. Would you rather have your brakes work very fast sometimes and very slowly sometimes, or would you rather know exactly how long it will take your brakes to respond each time?

Memory management is a particularly difficult problem in embedded operating systems. On one hand, embedded operating systems usually run on very minimal hardware, which has little or no hardware support for complex memory management. On the other hand, the "predictable" and "deterministic" requirements for real-time operating systems actually increase the need for complex memory management. Two simultaneous processes running in shared memory space can corrupt one another and crash both processes. Solving this problem—that is, how to have protected memory on minimal hardware—is one of the difficulties of RTOS design.

Linux/UNIX

The term *Linux* is often used as an umbrella term to mean "Linux and a whole lot of other things." Linux itself is simply the operating system *kernel*, the core parts of the software necessary to manipulate the hardware, control processes, and create a very basic user interface. In general, when somebody talks about Linux, they usually mean a Linux kernel and a collection of tools. Since many of these tools were created by the GNU Project, some people call a standard Linux installation GNU/Linux, but this terminology is rare.

Linux contains many powerful OS features, including multitasking (the ability to do multiple tasks at once), threads, virtual memory, loadable device driver modules, and networking.

Open Source

Open source might be a movement, an ideology, or a business plan, but in its simplest formation, open source is about licensing. An open source product is one that is distributed under a license that allows the right to read, redistribute and sell, modify, and freely use the source code and software.

Need to Know… Open Source

There are many different theories about why open source is good. The GNU Project (www.gnu.org) calls its software "free software" and not "open source," using open source innovator Richard Stallman's formulation: "free as in 'free speech,' not as in 'free beer.'" This group's philosophy is ideological: They believe that information deserves liberty and that it is morally wrong to have restrictive licenses. The Open Source Initiative, or OSI (www.opensource.org), has a much more pragmatic philosophy: They believe that reliable and high-quality code will be produced by the independent peer review that is fostered by open licenses. Although the two organizations have fundamentally different motivations for their support of free software and open source, the results are very similar. The Open Source Initiative's qualifications for certifying a software license as "OSI Certified" result in licenses that, for the most part, the more ideological GNU Project approves of.

Linux is by far the most successful open source operating system in use. It isn't the only one by a long shot, however. FreeBSD, OpenBSD, and NetBSD are other successful open source platforms, and Darwin, the BSD-based operating system that lies underneath MacOS X, is open source as well!

Software designed for one Linux distribution will probably work on another—as long as both distributions are using the same tools, libraries, and compilers. For this reason, building software on a Linux system can occasionally be very frustrating. Because Linux systems are so powerfully modular—that is, because each system can be running different versions of the various software components as needed—the Linux system in front of you might look very different from the Linux system in front of me. This is where the various distributions really show their strengths. If the user can say, "I'm using Debian 3.0. Does your product work on that?", compatibility tests are made far simpler.

History

In the late 1960s, some developers at Bell Labs started working on a project they called UNIX®, an outgrowth of an earlier Bell Labs project called Multics. UNIX was a powerful operating system with very useful features, and other development teams—primarily at the University of California, Berkeley—began work on their own versions, fiddling with and improving AT&T's code. The Berkeley operating system was powerful and robust and quickly became popular, but users still needed to purchase a license for the base code from AT&T (owners of Bell Labs). The licenses from AT&T became more and more expensive, and in 1989, the developers at Berkeley separated out most of the code that they had written themselves and which was not subject to the AT&T license. They released that code separately in what became the first of the freely redistributable software licenses. They quickly followed this release with a complete rewrite of what became known as *BSD*, which was a UNIX derivative written entirely from scratch and therefore no longer bound by the AT&T license.

NEED TO KNOW...

The source code to the original AT&T UNIX® is now owned by SCO, but the trademark to the word *UNIX* is owned by The Open Group. The many UNIX derivatives that exist need to avoid trademark violation. They tend to call themselves things like "UNIX-like," "*NIX," "UN*X," or "UNIX-variant." In everyday speech, users tend to refer to them all as "UNIX," but the trademark does exist.

Meanwhile, on the East Coast, Richard Stallman at MIT had spent the 1980s developing GNU (the recursive acronym stands for *GNUs not Unix*), a collection of programs and development tools that run on UNIX systems and variants. Licensed under the *GNU Public License* (*GPL*), all of the GNU Project's tools are freely modifiable and redistributable. Hackers went to work improving and fine-tuning those original programs, and before long, the GNU variants of most available tools for UNIX derivatives were more powerful than commercially released variants. By the late 1980s, the GNU Project had produced enough tools that they had almost an entire operating system. The only thing that they were missing was a kernel of their own.

Enter Linus Torvalds. In 1991, he was a student at the University of Helsinki in Finland. Inspired by the operating system Minix, a simple kernel that had been designed by Andrew Tannenbaum to teach operating system concepts to students, Linus began work on his own kernel. He released his new kernel, which he called Linux, under the GPL, and posted it on the Internet for suggestions and code review. Linux was designed to run with the existing GNU utilities, and quickly grew into the robust system that is widely used today. You could argue that with all of the effort that developers have put into the Linux kernel, the GNU utilities, and the accompanying tools, your typical Linux distribution is the product of the collective brainpower of the Internet working together for a common goal. And you would be right.

Embedded Linux (uCLinux)

Linux's appeal for designers of embedded systems rests in two of its core features: its open licensing and its modularity. Because it is an open source product, companies that are trying to keep costs down find Linux attractive, especially compared with the ever-increasing licensing demands of proprietary products. Additionally, a Linux installation can be very small. A basic installation of Linux can contain just the kernel and a few necessary device drivers. Because Linux is so modular, it is a trivial matter to strip away those parts of the OS that the embedded system designer doesn't need, leaving the final running system compact and efficient. Linux also runs on nearly every microprocessor in existence, which makes it extremely attractive for developers who want some flexibility in their hardware choices.

On the downside, standard Linux is not designed as a real-time operating system and is lacking the level of process interrupts that allow the operating system to behave deterministically. Some effort has gone into improving the process management for real-time versions of Linux to allow true interruptibility. Right now, the real upside for using Linux on an embedded system is its price and extensibility.

Programmers have made Linux run on diverse hardware platforms, from traditional computers such as Macintosh and Sparc to consumer electronic devices such as the iPod, Xbox, PlayStation 2, and PalmPilot PDA. For one example, see the Linux Xbox project (http://xbox-linux.sourceforge.net) More information on the uCLinux development community is available online at www.uclinux.org and www.ucdot.org.

Product Examples: Linux on Embedded Systems

Here are some products that use embedded versions of Linux :

- TiVo (Digital Video Recorder—but you knew this one)
- Sharp Zaurus (line of PDAs)

- G.Mate Yopy (PDA with games and music ability)
- Motorola A760 Linux/Java handset/PDA (PDA, cell and speaker phone, digital camera, video player, MP3 player)
- Panasonic broadband terminal/IP phone (Internet phone with Voice over IP)
- Dream-Multimedia-TV's Dreambox (digital radio, cable and satellite receiver, digital video recorder)
- Philips iPronto (home entertainment system control, home electronic control)
- empeg car audio player (car MP3 stereo)
- Mercedes-Benz UMTS test car (a navigation, Internet access, and game center module that has not yet been released—but when it is, *do not* try to hack the software on your car.

VxWorks

VxWorks is a commercial product made by Wind River Systems (www.windriver.com) that is used in many consumer electronic devices. VxWorks has a multitasking kernel with pre-emptive scheduling, as is appropriate for RTOS.

VxWorks interprocess communications are swift, and its memory management is relatively efficient. It can support multiple processors and has a simple debugger. Because it is designed strictly for embedded systems, VxWorks programs are written on a standard platform, compiled into VxWorks programs, and ported over to the VxWorks systems.

Wind River provides a commercial development toolkit with integrated compilers, debuggers, and other tools. A developer can also choose to use a standard C or C++ compiler rather than the VxWorks Developer's Toolkit. VxWorks is most well-known for being the OS controlling NASA's Mars PathFinder.

Windows Embedded

Microsoft Windows, the ubiquitous OS for desktop PCs, is also available in a leaner form for mobile devices and embedded systems. Microsoft Windows 1.0 was introduced in 1985, but it wasn't until the release of Windows 3.1 in 1992 and Windows 3.11 (Windows for Workgroups) in 1993 that the windowing system built on top of MS-DOS started to become widely used. In 1993, Microsoft also started releasing its Windows NT line and began to pave its way into the corporate market by providing a set of graphically administered tools that eased security, control, and file sharing for corporate users.

In 1996, Microsoft entered the embedded operating systems market with the first release of Windows CE. The current release of Windows CE, referred to as Windows CE .NET, has now been joined by Windows XP Embedded, a modularized version of the popular desktop version of Windows. Both are now developed in .NET, Microsoft's framework for application development. A developer can use Visual Studio .NET as the programming environment and can write code in:

- Microsoft Visual Basic
- Visual C++
- Visual C#
- Visual J#
- JScript
- A selection of approved third-party tools

Windows XP Embedded is intended for larger, complex systems, whereas Windows CE .NET is intended for smaller, less complex RTOS applications. Windows CE is also the OS used in Pocket PC-based PDAs, made by a variety of hardware manufacturers, provided they conform to Microsoft's guidelines.

Concepts

Windows CE is attractive to developers because of the familiar Windows-style interface it gives users. More importantly, because Windows CE includes a subset of the Win32 API, porting limited functionality versions of existing Windows programs becomes possible.

Windows CE is a preemptive multitasking operating system. Multiple processes can be running at one time, with each process running in a protected section of memory. A process consists of one or more threads, each with a different scheduling priority. Because Windows CE is real time, it needs to guarantee that events are noticed quickly. To do this, there is a high-priority *interrupt thread* running at all times, to catch events and schedule responses appropriately.

Windows CE is also an OS used in pocket PC-based PDAs, made by a variety of hardware manufacturers, provided they conform to Microsoft's guidelines.

Windows CE has a hierarchical architecture, with its various components layered on top of one another. In its simplified form, the lowest layer, the OEM Abstraction Layer (or OAL, and also known as the Hardware Abstraction Layer), is responsible for interfacing the device hardware to the Windows CE kernel. The OAL receives a version of the kernel tailored for a specific microprocessor and implements low-level hardware-specific code for power management, real-time clock, timers, and interrupt handling. The next layer is the subset of the Win32 API that handles graphics and windowing, communication, and other basic kernel functionality. The top layer consists of user applications.

Windows CE makes extensive networking and communications capabilities available to the programmer, providing access to standard wired and wireless communications. Typically, Windows CE applications are developed using the .NET tools on a standard Windows machine and are then tested using Windows CE-base software emulators.

NEED TO KNOW...

Windows CE supports an extensive range of communication protocols that allow your Windows CE device to communicate with other systems:

- **Networking features** Protected Extensible Authentication Protocol (PEAP), firewall, Network Driver Interface Specification (NDIS) 5.1, utilities, Universal Plug and Play (UPnP), VoIP, TCP/IP, TCP/IPv6.
- **Local Area Network (LAN)** 802.11, 802.1x, 802.3, 802.5, Wireless Protected Access (WAP).
- **Personal Area Network (PAN)** Bluetooth, Infrared Data Association (IrDA).
- **Wide Area Network (WAN)** Dial-up networking, point-to-point, telephony API, virtual private networking (VPN).
- **Servers** File Transfer Protocol (FTP), file and print, Simple Network Time Protocol (SNTP), Telnet, Web server.

Product Examples: Windows CE on Embedded Systems

- Alva MPO 5500 mobile phone/PDA (PDA aimed at the visually impaired)
- BSquare Power Handheld (PDA)
- Gotive H41 mobile communicator (PDA, cell phone, GPS, and barcode reader)
- iPAQ Pocket PC h5550 (PDA)
- Neonode N1 "limitless" mobile device (PDA, cell phone, digital camera, came device, jukebox, and remote control)
- Bernina artista 200E (sewing machine—yes, we're serious. The sewing machine industry is extremely high-tech these days.
- Hitachi Wearable Internet Appliance, or WIA (Head-mounted wearable computer with a tiny screen that flips over your eye.

Summary

Understanding the operating software of a computer or electronic device is much more difficult than it seems at first glance. Yet it's also very rewarding. Think about how much fun you'll have when you connect some strange old legacy bit of hardware to your PDA, or when you manage to make your TiVo do strange and glorious tricks. There's too much variation on types of hardware to give you more than the roughest overview in this chapter, but we hope we've given you a good introduction to what you can do.

In electronic devices and computer systems, operating systems are a key function that provide a layer of abstraction between user program and actual hardware. This chapter has provided a basic introduction to the concepts of operating systems as well as to a few specific OSs that should be useful in your hacking projects.

Additional Reading

- ***Modern Operating Systems,* by Andrew Tannenbaum (Pearson, 2001)** A good place to start if you are interested in more detailed information on the topic of OSs.
- **Embedded Systems Programming: www.embedded.com** This site has general Internet resources and links about embedded systems.
- **Microsoft Windows Embedded Developer Center: http://ms.dn.microsoft.com/embedded.**
- **Windows Devices: www.windowsdevices.com** Provides links, articles, and forums about Embedded Windows.
- **Linux Devices: www.linuxdevices.com** Provides great links, articles, and forums about Embedded Linux.
- **μCLinux-Embedded Linux Microcontroller Project: www.uclinux.org.**
- **Embedded Linux and μCLinux Developer Forum: www.ucot.org.**

Chapter 4

Coding 101

Topics in this chapter:

- **Programming Concepts**
- **Introduction to C**
- **Introduction to Debugging**
- **Introduction to Assembly Language**

Introduction

Programming languages are essential to all computers. The electrical components provide the infrastructure and the operating system gives us a framework to play in, but without programs, a computer is just a whirring chunk of plastic and metal. To be understood, a program needs to be written in a some programming language or another, just as a book is written in English or Japanese or Esperanto.

Most programming languages are *imperative* languages. In an imperative language, we give the computer a set of instructions and all the steps necessary to execute those instructions. Programming languages sit on a spectrum that ranges from *low-level* to *high-level*. It's not negative to call something a low-level language—it just means that the lines of code are relatively close to the actual commands being executed at the hardware level. A high-level language has more layers of abstraction. When we program in a high-level language, our code might not look at all like the actual instructions being executed by the computer. A compiler or interpreter takes care of converting our code into instructions the computer can understand. This chapter discusses programming from high-level C to low-level assembly, peeling each layer away like the layers of an onion.

Need to Know… Limitations of This Chapter

This chapter will not to turn you into a C or assembly language programmer. But it will teach you enough about the structures of these two languages so that you can start to find your way around. Most high-level languages you'll encounter will feel very similar to C and will differ primarily in the specific commands and syntax. If you ever need to learn an *object-oriented* language such as Java, you'll have some extra concepts to study, but many of the basic principles will be the same. If you want to do more advanced programming in these languages, look at the suggestions for further reading at the end of this chapter. You'll find yourself writing complex programs in no time!

Programming Concepts

In this section, we explore some of the essential concepts necessary for any programming language:

- Assignment
- Control structures (looping, conditional branching, and unconditional branching)
- Storage structures (structures, arrays, hash tables, and linked lists)
- Readability (comments, function and variable names, and pretty printing)

These concepts will serve you well for the specific programming languages we're learning here: C and assembly language. But, they are also important general concepts you'll need in any language you might learn, such as C++, Java, or Perl.

Assignment

Assignment occurs when your program stores some information in memory so you can use it later. To get to the information, you need some kind of handle for later access. Frequently we use *named variables*.

Let's say we would like to greet the user of our program by name. We might write a program that stores the user's name in a variable called <*name*>. The command to print the greeting might look something like:

```
print out "Hello, <name>."
```

When the program runs, the computer will recognize <*name*> as a named variable and will look in its memory in the spot labeled *name* to find the character string. The variable corresponds to the string *Buffy* in the example shown in Figure 4.1. The computer will then perform variable substitution and put the string *Buffy* where it saw the name of the variable:

```
Hello, Buffy.
```

Figure 4.1 Variable Assignment

Chunk of computer's memory labeled *name*
"Buffy"

Many programming languages make you *declare* variables before you use them for the first time. To declare a variable is to tell the program "I intend to use a variable with a certain name and of a certain type." Declarations allow the program to set aside enough space in memory to store all your variables.

Need to Know… Variable Declarations in Pseudocode

Programming languages have different ways of declaring and using named variables, some of which are introduced in this chapter. The <*variable-name*> syntax we use is one you'll often see in *pseudocode*. Pseudocode is a way of presenting coding examples if you aren't sure that all your readers will be using the same programming language or if you don't want to worry about whether or not you are placing the commas and semicolons in exactly the right places. You can't compile or run pseudocode, but if you know a programming language, you can easily convert a pseudocode example into a real example in the programming language you know. Pseudocode works because most imperative programming languages share the same features. The examples in this section are written in pseudocode.

If our name greeting example were written in C, it would appear as follows:

```
#include <stdio.h>

main()
{
        /* Initialize the user's name */
        char name[] = "Buffy";

        /* Print the user's name */
        printf("Hello, %s\n", name);
}
```

Control Structures

It would be pretty difficult to write a program if we had to tell the computer every single instruction and exactly when we wanted the computer to implement that instruction. Say we wanted to write a program to display the words "Hello, world" on the computer screen. If we had to tell the computer every instruction, our program might look something like this:

```
Print out "H".
Move the cursor right a few pixels.
Print out "e".
Move the cursor right a few pixels.
Print out "l".
...
```

The same program would be written in C as follows:

```
#include <stdio.h>

main()
{
        printf("H");
        printf("e");
        printf("l");
        ...
}
```

Even this simple program assumes that the computer already knows how to display each letter on the screen! To make programming easier, languages use looping, conditional branching, and unconditional branching.

Looping

Looping allows you to execute the same lines of code multiple times. Perhaps you want to say "Hello, world" five times. You could write the line of code *print out 'hello, world'* five times, or you could use a looping structure to tell your program to run your one line of code multiple times:

```
five times, print out 'hello, world'
```

Which would produce the output:

```
hello, world
hello, world
hello, world
hello, world
hello, world
```

This program would be written in C as follows:

```
#include <stdio.h>

main()
{
      int counter;    /* initialize the counter to integer */

      for ( counter = 0; counter < 5 ; counter++ )
               printf("hello, world\n");
}
```

Conditional Branching

Conditional branching allows you to tell your program what to do if certain conditions are met. For example, we might write a program that says goodbye to you at the end of the day. At 5:00 P.M. Monday through Thursday, we want our program to say "Goodnight. See you tomorrow!" But at 5:00 P.M. Friday, we want our program to say "Have a great weekend!" Our pseudocode might look something like:

```
If today is Monday, Tuesday, Wednesday, or Thursday, then print out "Goodnight. See
you tomorrow!"

Or

If today is Friday, then print out "Have a great weekend!"
```

This program would be written in C as follows:

```
#include <stdio.h>

main()
{
        char weekday;

        /*
         * Some code goes here to set "weekday" based on the current day
         */

         switch (weekday)
         {
         case 'M', 'T', 'W', 'R':
                printf("Goodnight. See you tomorrow!\n");
                break;
         case 'F':
                printf("Have a great weekend!\n");
                break;
         };     /* Finished with the switch statement */
}
```

The most common conditional branching structures are *if/then/else* statements, like the one in this example, and conditionals built into *loops* (which execute some lines of code until the following conditions are met).

Unconditional Branching

Unconditional branching allows you to tell your program what to do when a certain line is reached, without any conditions. Some blocks of code might be run many times. Unconditional branching allows you to write that frequently used code in some convenient location outside the main body of your program, storing it as a *procedure* or *function*. When you need to execute that block of code, you can branch to that block wherever it exists.

Here's an example:

```
<planet> = world                    [comment: assignment]
for five times
        print out "hello <planet>"
finish loop                         [comment: looping]
call function <day>                 [comment: unconditional branching]
begin function <day>
      if today is monday
              print out "happy monday"
      else
              print out "aren't you glad it isn't monday?"
      finish if                     [comment: conditional branching]
finish function <day>
```

If run on a Monday, this program will display:

```
hello world
hello world
hello world
hello world
hello world
happy monday
```

This might seem a bit complicated. On the other hand, this program would be written in C as follows:

```
#include <stdio.h>
main()
{
      int counter;                  /* declaration */
      char planet[] = "world";      /* declaration & assignment*/
      char today;                   /* declaration */
      void day();                   /* function declaration */
```

```
        for ( counter = 0; counter < 5; counter++ )
        {
                printf("hello %s\n", planet);
        }                              /* finished looping */

        day();                         /* unconditional branching */
}

void day()
{
        /*
         * Some code goes here to set "weekday" based on the current day
         */
        if (today == 'M')
        {
            printf("happy monday\n");
        }
        else  /* conditional branching */
        {
             printf("aren't you glad it isn't monday?\n");
        }
};
```

Storage Structures

When a computer program is running, it is usually processing large amounts of information. It stores that information in the computer's memory. The problem for a computer programmer is how best to store the information. If every piece of information the program needs were just written willy-nilly into the computer's memory, it would be very difficult for the programmer to recall that information when it is needed—not to mention slow for the computer to find it! To solve this problem, programmers use *storage structures*—software components that simplify information storage. These structures are sometimes symbolic, existing primarily in your mind as you write your code, without your programming language being aware of them. We'll see more how this works when we look at C in more detail.

Four of the most important storage structures are:

- Structures
- Arrays
- Hash tables
- Linked lists

Need to Know… A Note About Storage Structures, C, and Assembly Language

Hash tables and linked lists are high-level data structures and are not built in to any standard implementations of C or assembly language. Many C programs include homegrown implementations of linked lists and hash tables (which are fairly easy to write) because they are so useful. We can't teach you the details of every implementation, but we can teach you enough about the basics to recognize them and to know how to use them when you see them.

Structures

Before we go into details about the various storage structures, let's start with the miscellaneous storage structure: the appropriately named *structure* (see Figure 4.2). Structures (sometimes called *records*) are conglomerations of different types of data. For example, a pizza recipe structure might hold:

- An array (illustrated in Table B.1) of ingredients to make the crust
- A linked list (as illustrated in Table B.4) of ingredients to make the toppings
- One bowl
- One oven

Figure 4.2 A Pizza Recipe Structure, With Elements We'll Explore in More Detail Shortly

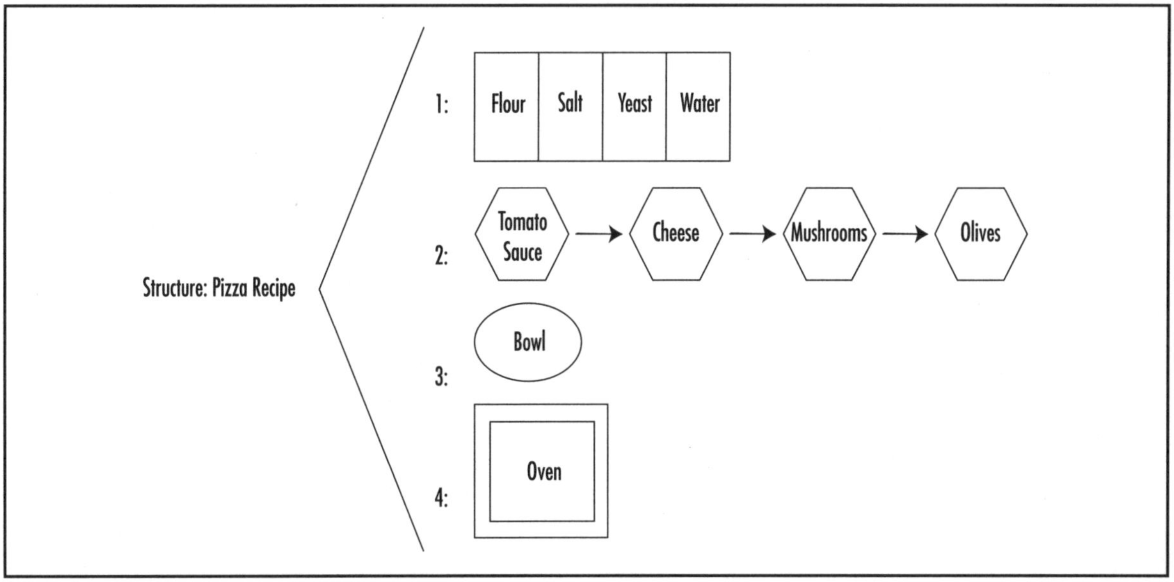

Structures are handy mostly as a logical organization aid. In a large and complex program, you might use a structure to make it easier for you to remember what data should be treated as part of one logical unit.

Arrays

One way of storing data is in an *array*. An array is like a long row of post office boxes. Each post office box has a unique number on its door and contains mail for one person or family. When a post office customer wants to check her mail, she looks in the box with her number on the door. Her mail is always stored in that box.

In an array, the computer cordons off an area of memory that holds the information being stored, just like the post office wall is filled with post office boxes. Each virtual post office box is called an *array element*. Each element stored in the array is indexed by a number. If you want to retrieve the information stored in the fourth chunk of the array, for example, you would request the information telling the computer the array's name and the chunk you want to retrieve. For example, your array might be called *crust* and contain all the different ingredients for pizza crust. An example of array *crust* is shown in Table 4.1.

Table 4.1 The Sample Array *crust*

The Array crust	
element 1	flour
element 2	salt
element 3	yeast
element 4	water

Now *crust (4)* contains the string *water*. Your pseudocode program might say:

```
print to screen "add " + crust(4)
```

which would produce the output:

```
add water
```

Need to Know… A Note About Numbering

In most programming languages, numbering actually starts at 0, not at 1. A list with four elements will have those elements numbered 0, 1, 2, and 3. So the array in Table 4.1 will actually look more like the array shown in Table 4.2.

Table 4.2 Correctly Numbered Array *crust*

Array crust	
element 0	flour
element 1	salt
element 2	yeast
element 3	water

There are four numbers there, but the first one is numbered 0 and the last one is numbered 3.

Hash Tables

If you live in a very small town, you might not need post office boxes, because the postmaster knows every resident of the town by sight. Instead of going into the post office, walking up to a large wall full of numbered boxes, and fetching all the mail in the box numbered "303", you just walk up to the postmaster's desk and say "Hi, Clark! I'm picking up Chloe's mail today. Does she have anything?" To which the postmaster replies, "Good morning, Lex! Here's Chloe's mail." Instead of requesting Chloe's mail by the number of her box, you requested by her name. This is how *hash tables* work. In a hash table, your elements are not indexed by number, as they are in an array, but by a unique name, or *key*. This is illustrated in Table 4.3.

Table 4.3 The Sample Hash Table *Greetings*

Key	Output
English	hello
French	bonjour
Russian	zdravstvuite
Spanish	hola

Your pseudocode program might say:

```
print to screen greetings(Spanish) + "world!"
```

Which would produce the output:

```
hola world!
```

Need to Know… Hash Tables Versus Arrays

You might ask why we don't always use hash tables instead of arrays. After all, isn't it easier to remember that the Spanish word for hello is stored in the box keyed with the word *Spanish* than it is to remember that it's box number 4? There are two answers to this question. First, in this example, it *is* easier to remember *Spanish* than 4. But more importantly, arrays are nearly always faster than hash tables. This speed of hash table access and array access varies among different language implementations, but it is usually much faster for the computer to find array elements. See the discussion of array implementation in C for an example of why this is usually so.

Linked Lists

Hash tables and arrays are all well and good if you're going to be accessing one piece of information at a time, as if you were fetching your mail from a post office box. But maybe you need to get at your stored information in a particular order, first one piece, and then the next. For example, you've decided to make a pizza from scratch. You need to start with flour, salt, yeast, and water, and then later add tomato sauce, cheese, mushrooms, and garlic. You have to make sure you access your ingredients in order because it won't be a very good pizza if you mix the flour with the mushrooms. A *linked list* makes sure that you access the ingredients in order—a detail that it has in common with arrays. The main difference between an array and a linked list is that in a linked list, you can add or remove containers from your list. Remember, an array is like a wall of post office boxes. If you are storing the ingredients for your pizza in a wall of post office boxes, your pizza recipe might look similar to Table 4.4.

Table 4.4 Array of Pizza Ingredients

1	2	3	4	5	6	7	8
Flour	Salt	Yeast	Water	Tomato sauce	Cheese	Mushrooms	Olives

But what if you decide that you don't want mushrooms on your pizza? You can take the mushrooms out of box 7, but there's still an empty post office box between the cheese and the olives. That's both wasteful and confusing and would lead to an arrangement similar to Table 4.5.

Table 4.5 Modified Array of Pizza Ingredients

1	2	3	4	5	6	7	8
Flour	Salt	Yeast	Water	Tomato sauce	Cheese		Olives

Worse, what if you learn that your pizza crust will be much tastier if you add some egg to the dough? In order to fit in the egg after the water, you'll need to shift the water to box 5, the tomato sauce to box 6, and so on down the line, all just to put the eggs into box 4. Not very practical!

This is why in kitchens we keep our ingredients in ingredient bowls, not in post office boxes. If we have eight ingredient bowls on the kitchen counter, and we decide we don't want mushrooms on the pizza, we can toss out the seventh bowl and move the olives closer to the cheese. If we decide to add eggs, we can squeeze a bowl of eggs between the bowl of yeast and the bowl of water. This arrangement is illustrated in Figure 4.3.

Figure 4.3 Linked-List Pizza Crust Ingredients

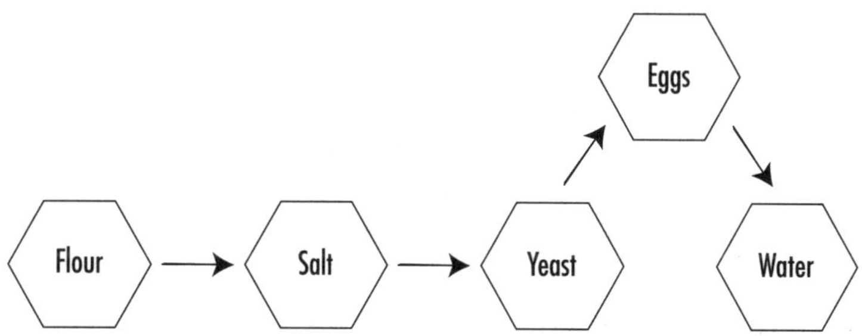

This is how linked lists work. When we need a new container for information, we can slip one in between two prior containers. When we need to delete an information container, we can do that, too. The disadvantage of linked lists is that we can't directly access a container: "Fetch me the fourth ingredient." We have to say "Fetch me the next ingredient" or (in some implementations) "Fetch me the previous ingredient." Pseudocode for baking a pizza might look like this:

```
while there is a next bowl after this one,
      fetch me the current ingredient;
      empty the bowl, and move to the next bowl;
when there isn't a next bowl after this one,
     empty the current bowl, and put the pizza in the oven.
```

Readability

In order to make code maintainable—to fix its bugs and update it as time passes—you should make sure your code is as readable as possible. Programmers joke about code that is *WORN* (Write Once, Read Never). It's easy to write a computer program that is completely unreadable. But unless you're trying to win the annual International Obfuscated C Contest (a genuine contest, run since 1984, which gives prizes to the most unreadable and bizarre C program entered—archives available at www.ioccc.org/years-spoiler.html), you probably want to make sure that you can read your own code after you've written it.

Comments

All computer languages give you the ability to write *comments* in the code. Comments are blocks of the program text that the computer ignores. Comments are intended for you, the programmer, and anyone else who might need to read the code. Since computer languages rarely look much like English, it can be difficult to look at a piece of code you've written after some time has passed and understand exactly what it does. If you include comments explaining the intent of each significant block of code, you'll always be able to understand the original intent of those lines. Each language has a different way of telling the computer that some lines of text are comments and not program code, such as the symbols # , /*, or //, but it is usually pretty easy to recognize them. An example of commenting is shown in Figure 4.4.

Figure 4.4 Pseudocode With Comments

```
while nextBowl exists         /* if the next bowl isn't empty */
      fetch Ingredient        /* take the ingredient from the current bowl */
      nextBowl                /* move to the next bowl */
      delete prevBowl         /* put the previous, empty bowl in the sink */

when nextBowl doesn't exist   /* when you're done, */
      delete Bowl             /* put the last bowl in the sink */
      bake pizza              /* and put the pizza in the oven! */
```

Function and Variable Names

When you're writing a computer program, you'll probably have the opportunity to assign lots of arbitrary names to variables and functions. It's easy to get lazy and assign function and variable names that are very short, so you don't have to type very much. But take a look at the program from Figure 4.4 if we replace all the variable names with something very short and easy to type, as shown in Figure 4.5.

Figure 4.5 Psuedocode With Confusing Variable Names

```
while i exists              /* if the next bowl isn't empty */
      fetch k               /* take the ingredient from the current bowl */
      i                     /* move to the next bowl */
      delete m              /* put the previous, empty bowl in the sink */

when i doesn't exist        /* when you're done, */
      delete j              /* put the last bowl in the sink */
      bake n                /* and put the pizza in the oven! */
```

This piece of pseudocode means the same thing as far as the computer is concerned, but it doesn't really make any sense to you or me. Whenever possible, use variable and function names that have meaning to you in the context of your program. Doing so might involve a little bit more typing now, but it will make your life much, much easier later, when you have to fix a bug in your code.

White Space

In most modern programming languages, an excess of white space is ignored by the computer. This means that you can use as many—or as few—tabs and space characters as you need. Your program will be easier to read later if you format it so that it is clear how the program flows. When it comes to the nitty-gritty details of formatting, there are as many preferences as there are programmers. However, a couple of broad conventions have been agreed on as generally useful:

- Use a new line to indicate a new command. Figure 4.4 could have been written in just two lines, but it would have been much harder to read:

  ```
  while nextBowl exists; fetch Ingredient; nextBowl; delete prevBowl.
  when nextBowl doesn't exist; delete Bowl; bake pizza.
  ```

- If a block of text is part of a loop, function, or conditional structure, use leading white space to show the lines of code that are being evaluated similarly. Here is the pseudocode from Figure 4.4 without leading white space for the loop and conditional statements. This is much harder to read than the sample with white space:

  ```
  while nextBowl exists
  fetch Ingredient
  nextBowl
  delete prevBowl
  when nextBowl doesn't exist
  delete Bowl
  bake pizza
  ```

Introduction to C

C is a runtime environment that exists on nearly every computer platform. C is a platform-independent compiled language, but it has a large library of hardware-specific, low-level system calls available to help us access the hardware that we are programming for. On its own, C is a very small language; it doesn't even know how to display text to the screen! But every C installation comes with the C *standard libraries*, which provide the programmer with a host of handy functions.

C is a *compiled* language. This means that we write the program in the English-like language that you're learning here and then use another program (a *compiler*) to convert it into commands the computer can understand and execute.

NEED TO KNOW... YOUR COMPILER

Many different C compilers are available. You might be using a command-line compiler, for which you write your program in a text editor such as Notepad, Emacs, or vi and then compile your program with a command such as *cc myprogram.c -o myprogram.exe*. You might be using a graphical programming environment, where you write and compile your program in an easy-to-understand window, such as Visual C or CodeWarrior. We can't teach you the ins and outs of the compiler you'll be using, because they're all different. Refer to your compiler manual for instructions on how to compile your C program.

History and Basics of C

C was invented by Dennis Ritchie (based on work done by Kenneth Thompson) in the early 1970s as a language intended for programming on Thompson's brand-new UNIX operating system. C was standardized into what we now know as *ANSI C* in the mid-1980s. For many years, C was primarily used for programming on UNIX and its variants, but it is now a widespread standard. C and its descendents (including C++ and C#) are among the most commonly used programming languages.

Printing to the Screen

A C program is just a sequence of commands. Let's start with our first program, the ubiquitous "hello, world," which is the first program you will learn to write in almost any programming language (see Figure 4.6).

Figure 4.6 The Hello, World Program

```
1       #include <stdio.h>
2
3       main()
4       {
5               printf("hello, world\n");
6       }
```

Let's break down this program. The meat of any C program, the part that runs when you execute the program, is the *main* block. This main block is a special-purpose *function* that tells your program to begin its work here. You can see the declaration of the main block on line 3 of Figure 4.6. Those parentheses after the word *main* are required after any function and are used to pass arguments to the function if you need any (we'll get to some details of function calls and argument passing later). In this program, we aren't passing any arguments to the main function, so the parentheses are present but empty.

After a function's initial line, all statements that belong to that function are grouped together with curly braces {}. In this program, those curly braces are on lines 4 and 6. Anything between those curly braces (in this case, line 5) is part of the function. So, in this program, the heart of the main block is the command on line 5:

```
printf("hello, world\n");
```

The command *printf*, like *main*, is a function. Notice that it begins with the function name (*printf*) followed by zero or more arguments in closing parentheses (in this case, one argument, which is equal to the string *"hello, world\n"*). *printf* is the formatted print command. Here it is printing to the screen the contents of its argument: the characters *hello world* followed by *\n*. In a C character string, a single character preceded by the backslash character (\) has a special meaning. *\n* is the C notation for printing a new line to the screen. You can't put a new line directly in a quoted string, for example:

```
"here is my first line
here is my second"
```

This is not valid C. To write those lines to the screen, your command would have to be:

```
printf("here is my first line\nhere is my second\n")
```

or a variant:

```
printf("here is my first line\n");
printf("here is my second\n");
```

or:

```
printf("here is ");
printf("my first line\nhere is my second\n");
```

The separate *printf* commands don't change where a new line begins. Only the *\n* characters create new lines.

Need to Know… Some Interesting Character String Escape Sequences

Several similar sequences cause *printf* to display something special to the screen. Some are very special types of characters, such as the audible alert bell that *printf* sounds when given the character sequence \a. Most are designed simply to escape the meaning of some other character (hence the name *escape sequences*), to allow *printf* to print the literal character instead of trying to interpret the meaning. For example, if we need to display a double quote mark (") on the screen, we need to prevent *printf* from parsing the special meaning of the double quote mark as "here is the beginning or end of a character string." Some of the more interesting escape sequences include:

- **\n** newline
- **\t** horizontal tab
- **\?** question mark
- **\'** single quote
- **\"** double quote
- **\a** alert bell

Earlier we mentioned that C doesn't really have much complex functionality of its own and doesn't even know how to output characters to the screen in any simple way. Well, that's where line 1 of Figure 4.6 comes in. C has standard libraries that provide that basic functionality that is not built into the language. To make your final program as small as possible, you include only the standard libraries you need into your program. Line 1 includes the standard library *stdio.h,* which is responsible for standard input and output functionality. The included library provides us with the *printf* function.

One last character we haven't covered: that semicolon (;) at the end of line 5. C commands are separated by semicolons, not by white space, so the following commands are legal:

```
printf("here is ");
printf("my first line\nhere is my second\n");
```

But this next example isn't:

```
printf("here is ")
printf("my first line\nhere is my second\n")
```

Data Types in C

C is a *strongly typed* language. This means that the language distinguishes among the different types of data it can process. It's important to recognize data types for many reasons. For one thing, your programming language needs to allocate storage for any information you intend to store. To store the integer 8 is relatively simple; you need as much space is the computer will take to store that integer. But what if you want to store the real number 8? (To program efficiently, you're going to use things you learned in math class! Remember that integers are only the numbers $-\infty,\ldots,-3,-2,-1,0,1,2,3,\ldots,\infty$, but that real numbers also include numbers like 3.759.) If you want to store the real number 8 to, say, three points of precision (that is, so you can distinguish between 8.000 and 8.003), you'll need a lot more storage space in the computer. And if you want to be able to distinguish between 8.000 and -8.000, you'll need even more space. So it's important to use the right data type for your variable, or you can rapidly run out of memory for your program.

C has only a few data types:

- **`int`** An integer.
- **`float`** A single precision floating-point number (basically, a real number).
- **`double`** A double precision floating-point number (basically, a real number with extra precision).
- **`char`** One character.

These data types can optionally be used with the following modifiers:

- **`short`** If you aren't using very large numbers and want the program to allocate space effectively.
- **`long`** If you are using very large numbers.
- **`signed`** If it matters to you whether the numbers are positive or negative.
- **`unsigned`** If you're not going to be using negative numbers and you want the program to allocate space effectively.

If you've done some programming before, you might notice two types that are missing here: Booleans and character strings. Booleans (the values *true* and *false*) are usually represented in C as a special case of integers. Character strings are arrays of characters. We'll talk more about how to implement character strings later.

Mathematical Functions

You know what's really great about computers? They know how to do arithmetic, so we don't have to. Many basic mathematical functions are included in C, and to use them you don't need to include any standard libraries. An additional library called *math.h* provides more complex mathematical functions such as sines, cosines, logarithms, and powers. Figure 4.7 displays a program that calculates the number of minutes in a day.

Figure 4.7 Mathematical Example

```
1    #include <stdio.h>
2
3    main()
4    {
5            /* variable declarations */
6            int seconds, minutes, hours;
7            int total;
8            seconds = 60;          /* number of seconds in one minute */
9            minutes = 60;          /* number of minutes in one hour */
10           hours = 24;            /* number of hours in one day */
11
12           total = seconds * minutes * hours;   /* calculate total */
13           printf("there are %d seconds in one day.\n", total);
14    }
```

When you run this program, your computer should print out the line:

```
there are 86400 seconds in one day.
```

Let's step through this program to see what we did. You recognize line 1—it includes the standard input and output library. We're using this library to get the *printf* command, which will print the results of our mathematical equation. Line 3 begins the main function, and line 4 provides the curly brace that tells the program "the lines between here and the matching curly brace belong in the main function."

The first new line we've seen in this program is on line 5: /* *variable declarations* */. This is a C comment: a line of the program that is there for your benefit only but is ignored by the compiler. Anything between the initial /* and the closing */ is a *comment* and not part of the program. The comment on line 5 lets us know that we are about to *declare variables*.

Variables in C are declared before use. A declaration, which consists of a data type and some number of variable names, tells the program the sort of information that is going to be stored in that variable. In Figure 4.7, the variables are defined in two lines (6 and 7):

```
int seconds, minutes, hours;
int total;
```

Because they're all of the same type (*int*—that is, integers), we could have declared them all in one line:

```
int seconds, minutes, hours, total;
```

or on four separate lines as follows:

```
int seconds;
int minutes;
int hours;
int total;
```

C doesn't care how you lay it out, so you should use whichever method makes your code most readable for you. You might split conceptually—variables that all refer to one function on one line and to another function on a second line—or by any other method you like.

After you've declared your variables, you can assign them. *Assignment* gives a value of the appropriate type to the variable you have even a declaration. In this case, the appropriate type is integer, so we assign each variable name its initial value as follows (lines 8, 9, and 10):

```
seconds = 60;
minutes = 60;
hours = 24;
```

This way before we begin the computation, the variables contain meaningful values.

On line 12, the actual calculation occurs:

```
total = seconds * minutes * hours;
```

Most of these characters should be fairly familiar:

- Equals sign (=) is the *assignment operator*, which places the results of the calculation to the right of the equals sign into the variable on the left.
- The asterisk (*) says to multiply, just like you would use × in a written calculation: seconds × minutes × hours.
- To add and subtract you would, predictably, use the plus sign (+) and the minus sign (-), and to divide, you would use the slash (/).

The statement on line 13 is a *printf* statement, but this one looks a little different. For one thing, it has two arguments separated by a comma: a quoted character string and a variable name.

```
printf("there are %d seconds in one day.\n", total);
```

The *printf* function does more than just output simple character strings to the screen. It can do complex output formatting. The first argument to the *printf* function is always a character string. That character string can contain some number of substitution characters, each one a letter prefaced by %. For each substitution character, the *printf* function takes an argument explaining which variable will have its contents substituted into the character string.

In this example, the substitution character is *%d*. This is C for "take the value of the variable for the corresponding argument and display it as a decimal integer." The argument that corresponds to *%d* is *total*. In the preceding calculation, the value of *total* was set to 60 * 60 * 24, or 86,400. Thus, the function's output will be:

```
there are 86400 seconds in one day.
```

NOTE

This non-intuitive removal of the variable from the printing string isn't present in some higher-level languages. In Java, for example, the preceding statement would be:

```
System.out.println("there are " + total + " seconds in one day.");
```

You might ask why we set the number of seconds in a minute, the number of minutes in an hour, and the number of hours in a day as variable values. After all, aren't variables supposed to be, well, variable? But there are always 60 seconds in one minute, always 60 minutes in one hour, and always 24 hours in one day. And in fact, there is a way to create a *symbolic constant* to hold this kind of information that will never change. Instead of declaring and assigning the following variable:

```
int seconds;
seconds = 60;
```

you can define a symbolic constant:

```
#define SECONDS 60
```

At compliation time, every occurrence of *SECONDS* will be replaced with your replacement text, *60*. Note that there is no semicolon completing a *#define* line. By convention, symbolic constants are written in all capital letters to distinguish them from variable names, which are conventionally some combination of upper- and lowercase letters.

Control Structures

Remember all those control structures we learned about the beginning of the chapter? Well, C can do all of those. We'll look at two forms of looping (*for* loops and *while* loops) and two forms of conditional branching (*if/then/else* statements and *switch* statements). Unconditional branching in C is implemented with function calls, which we'll deal with in the next section.

For Loops

The *for* statement is a loop that operates until a certain condition has been met. This concept is shown in Figure 4.8.

Figure 4.8 A Sample *for* Loop

```
int i;


for ( i = 1; i <= 10; i++ )
{
        ...
}
```

There are three components to the loop's control mechanism, all stored within the parentheses. Look at the three parts of the statement in Figure 4.8, separated by semicolons. First:

```
i = 1
```

This part of the loop initializes any variables that will be used during the loop's control. Here we are taking a variable *i* (which has been declared beforehand as an integer—*int i;*) and initializing it to 1. The second part of the *for* loop's control gives a test condition:

```
i <= 10
```

This test is evaluated during program operation. In this case it is asking whether or not the variable stored in *i* is less than or equal to 10. If it isn't, the program will exit this *for* loop and continue on with whenever it was doing before the loop was entered. If it is, the body of the loop will be executed. Before we re-enter the loop and perform all this once more, we do the third step of the *for* loop:

```
i++
```

This step increments the counter variable we are using in the loop. This command tells C to add 1 to the variable stored in *i*.

The first time this program runs, the variable *i* will be initialized to 1, the program will test to see if 1 is less than or equal to 10, and it will discover that it is. The body of the loop will be executed, the variable *i* will be incremented by the statement *i++* to 2, and the process will begin again. After the tenth time this program runs, the variable *i* will be incremented to 11, and the loop will stop as *i* no longer meets the test condition.

Comparison Operators and Increment/Decrement Operators

In this section you were introduced to two new operators: <=, a comparison operator, and ++, an increment operator.

Comparison operators test some relation between the value on the left and the value on the right:

- < Is less than.
- <= Is less than or equal to.
- > Is greater than.
- >= Is greater than or equal to.
- == Is equal to.
- != Is not equal to.

NOTE

To test if two values are equal, the comparison operator has two equals signs (= =). To assign a value to a variable, the assignment operator has one equals sign (=). Don't get them confused! If you accidentally write a comparison statement like *i = 10*, your statement won't test to see if the variable *i* is equivalent to 10; it will assign the value 10 to your variable.

Increment and *decrement operators* provide shorthand for adding or subtracting one to a variable:

- *i++, ++i,* and *i = i + 1* all add 1 to the value of *i.*
- *i--, --i,* and *i = i - 1* all subtract 1 from the value of *i.*

WARNING

Actually, the three forms do have subtly different meanings having to do with timing and precedence. These distinctions shouldn't matter at this level of programming, but be aware that they exist as you move on to more advanced programming tasks.

While Loops

A *while* loop is very similar to a *for* loop, but rather than having the variable initialization and incrementation controlled by the loop itself, they happen elsewhere. We *initialize* the variable before we ever enter the *while* loop, *test* the variable value in the loop control, and take care of any *variable modification* inside the body of the loop. The *for* loop in Figure 4.8 can be implemented with a *while* loop as shown in Figure 4.9.

Figure 4.9 A Sample *while* Loop

```
int i;
i = 1;

while ( i <= 10 )
{
        ...
        i++;
}
```

The counter variable is set before we begin the loop. When we enter the loop, we perform the test: Is the variable less than or equal to 10? If it is, we enter the loop, perform some code in the block, and finish incrementing the counter variable as part of the block.

If/Else

An *if* statement performs conditional branching. In an *if* statement, we test to see if the condition is true, do something if it is, and possibly do something else if it isn't. We've done tests as part of the *while* loops and *for* loops, but there is no looping built into *if* statements. An *if* statement might look similar to that shown in Figure 4.10.

Figure 4.10 A Sample *if/else* Statement

```
int i;
...
if ( i == 1 )
{
        [A: some lines of code here]
}
else if ( i == 2 )
        [B: only one statement can go here]
else
{
        [C: some lines of code here]
}        /* end if statement */
```

First, our *if* statement tests to see if the variable *i* is equivalent to 1. If it is, it executes the lines of code enclosed in the braces and terminates the statement (that is, no code in the *else* clauses of this statement will be executed). If it isn't, it looks to see if there is an *else* clause, and there is. The first *else* condition says to run another test: Is the variable equivalent to 2? If it is, we enter that block of code (notice that there are no braces around that next section of code; this is permissible as long as there is only one semicolon-terminated statement in the block) and don't execute any other *else* clauses in this *if* statement. If the variable isn't equivalent to 2, we move on to the final clause. Because there is no *if* after this final *else*, all other cases execute this block of code:

- If we enter the *if* statement when the variable *i* is equal to 1, we will execute only the line of code labeled *A*.
- If we enter the *if* statement when the variable *i* is equal to 2, we will execute only the line of code labeled *B*.
- If we enter the *if* statement when the variable *i* is equal to any number other than 1 or 2, we will execute only the line of code labeled *C*.

Switch

A *switch* statement is like a special case of a multi-tiered *if/else* statement. In each test of an *if* statement, you can test for something different. For example, you could write a program similar to Figure 4.11.

Figure 4.11 A Complex *if/else* Statement

```
if ( foo == 1 )
{
        ...
}
else if ( bar <= 39 )
{
        ...
}
else if ( baz == 's' )
{
        ...
}
```

But often your tests are much simpler than this and you just want to test for assorted values of a single variable (which is, in fact, what we did in Figure 4.10 to learn *if* statements). *Switch* statements deal with this special case of testing simply to see if one expression matches one of a number of values (see Figure 4.12).

Figure 4.12 A Sample *switch* Statement

```
switch (foo)
{
        case 1:
                 [A: some lines of code]
        case 2: case 5:
                 [B: some lines of code]
                break;
        default:
                 [C: some lines of code]
                break;
}
```

This code is running a test on the variable named *foo*. If the variable *foo* is equivalent to 2 or to 5 (the line *case 2: case 5:*), it will execute the lines of code we've marked *B* and then break out of the *switch* statement. If the variable *foo* is equivalent to 1 (the line *case 1:*), it will execute the lines of code we've marked *A*, but because there is no *break;* statement, *it will also execute the lines of code labeled* B. Be careful of this; remember to use *break*! If the variable *foo* is equivalent to any number other than 1, 2, or 5, it will execute the code labeled *default*, the code we've marked *C*.

NOTE

The lines of code after a "case" in a *switch* statement do not need curly braces around them. The switch statement itself does need curly braces.

Storage Structures

Arrays, Pointers, and Character Strings

A *pointer* is a special kind of variable. Its job is to contain the address of another variable. The address is the location in the computer's memory where the second variable lives. Your house address is a pointer to where on your street, in your town, you live. Knowing your address, we can come find you. Similarly, the variable's address tells the computer program how to find that variable in memory.

Pointers, and their cousins *address operators* and *arrays,* can be extremely powerful, but they can also be very confusing. Understanding pointers and dereferencing are the biggest hurdle in learning C.

They won't make sense all at once; don't worry, it will sink in over time! Once you master this concept, you'll be well on your way to becoming a great programmer.

To begin, let's imagine that we have an integer variable called *my_variable*. If we want a pointer to it, we can declare one using the ampersand (&) operator to find the address of *my_variable*. We begin by declaring the two variables, one integer and one pointer to integer:

```
int my_variable;

int *my_pointer;
```

The asterisk (*) in front of *my_pointer* defines *my_pointer* as a pointer to some other value. In this case, since the declaration begins *int* *, we know it's a pointer to a value of type *integer*. The pointer refers to some location in memory, with no value yet assigned (see Figure 4.13).

Figure 4.13 Declaring a Pointer

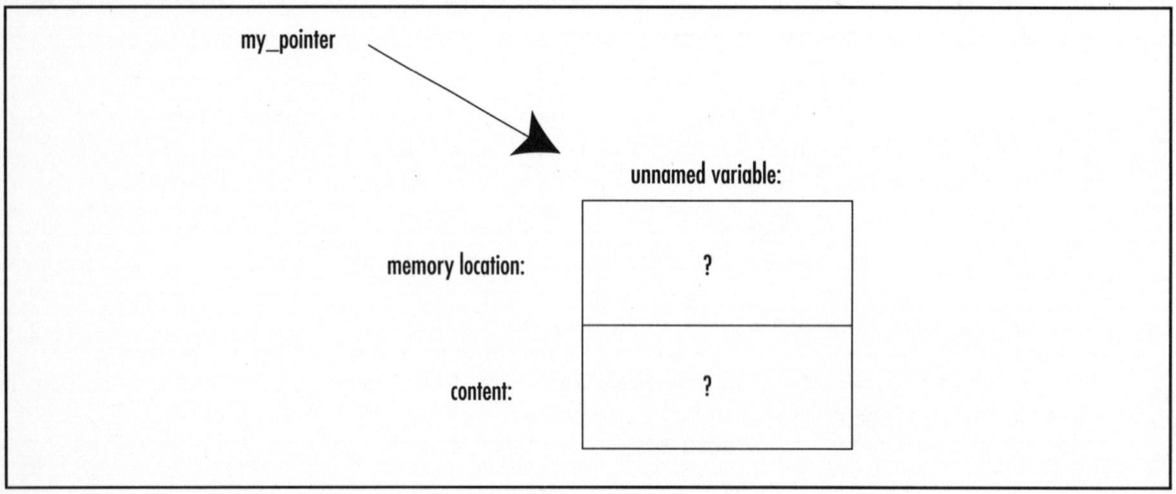

Now we follow the declaration with an assignment:

```
my_pointer = &my_variable;
```

Figure 4.14 illustrates this assignment. Though the integer named *my_variable* has no value yet, it does have an assigned memory location that's large enough to hold an integer value. The variable *my_pointer* points to *my_variable*. The ampersand (&) character in front of *my_variable* sends out the address of the memory location that has been set aside to store the variable's contents in this example, 0xBEEF1268. The assignment of this value to *my_pointer* means that *my_pointer* always knows the memory location of the variable held in that location. That is, *my_pointer* points to *my_variable*.

Figure 4.14 Assigning a Pointer to an Address of Another Variable

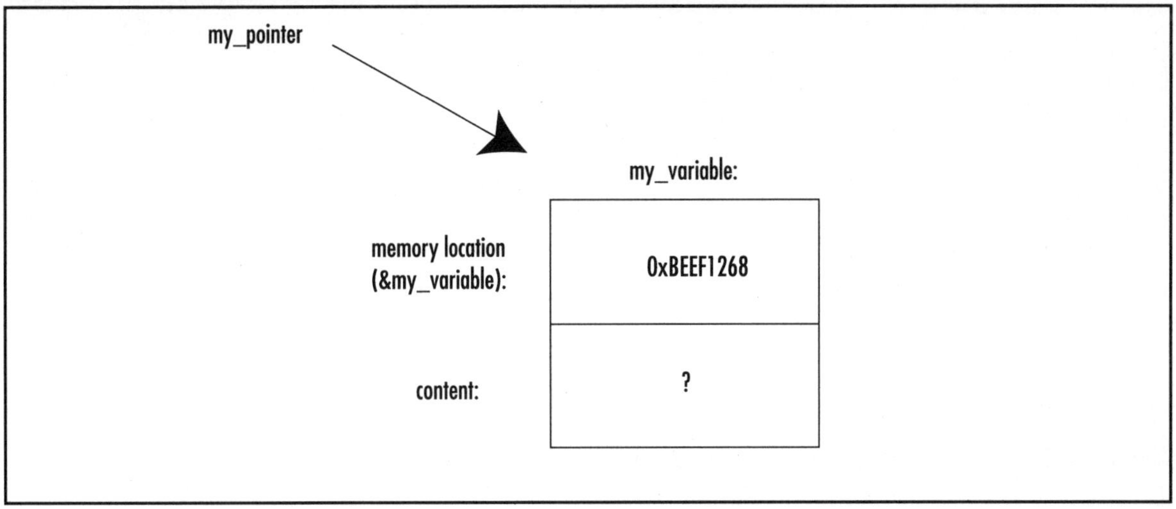

The integer stored in *my_variable* (and pointed to by *my_pointer*) can then be assigned into the location pointed at by *my_pointer*. Figure 4.15 illustrates the pointer once the value has been assigned with the command:

```
*my_pointer = 10;
```

Figure 4.15 Pointer Assignment

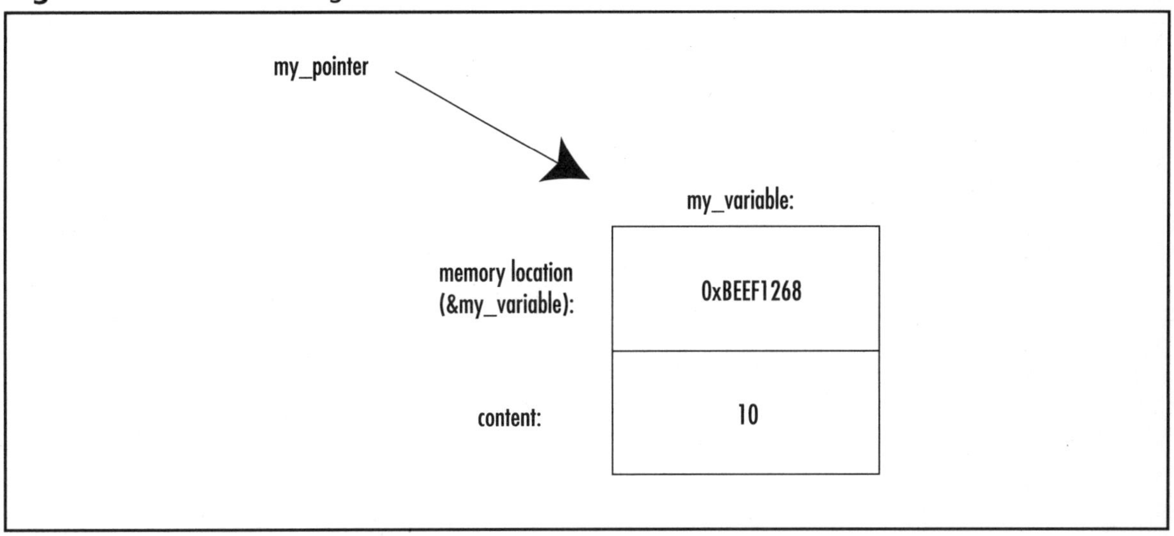

Note that when we are giving the address of the integer to *my_pointer* (*my_pointer = &my_variable*), we don't need to use the asterisk (*); we are assigning an address (obtained through the ampersand [&] operator) to a pointer variable, which takes an address without transformation. But when we give an actual integer value to *my_pointer* in with the command **my_pointer = 10*, we don't want to change the address of the thing that is being pointed to, but the thing itself, its content—so we need to use the asterisk (*) to show that extra level of indirection. The * character is called the *dereferencing* operator because it tells our code not to look at the address reference but at the object it points to, or references.

Arrays in C can be thought of as a special case of pointers. When you declare an array that contains 10 units in C, you're creating your array (like a row of post office boxes) in 10 consecutive chunks of memory.

As you can see in Table 4.6, the elements are referenced by the array name (*my_array*) and their locations in the array: *my_array[0], my_array[1],…, my_array[9]*.

Table 4.6 An Array Split up into Individual Pointers

Array my_array				
my_array[0]	my_array[1]	my_array[2]	my_array[3]	my_array[4]
my_array[5]	my_array[6]	my_array[7]	my_array[8]	my_array[9]

This is the most straightforward way to deal with arrays. But when you're looking at code other people have written, you might notice that they have declared arrays with pointers. See, there's a tricky little side effect in the direct memory addressing that pointers give you. We set up a pointer to the new array:

```
my_array_pointer = &my_array[0];
```

(which, in C shorthand, can also be written as *my_array_pointer = my_array;*—the name of the array is synonymous with the address of the first element). *my_array_pointer* is an address in memory. That address in memory points to the first element in 10 consecutive chunks of memory that comprise my array. So in a nifty and incredibly confusing operation called *pointer arithmetic*, you can access the second element of the array by saying:

```
*(my_array_pointer+1)
```

Confusing? As though that weren't bad enough, here's a new wrinkle: Declaring a pointer doesn't actually allocate enough memory for the entire array. If you decide to declare your arrays by using pointers instead of array notation, you'll have to learn how to allocate memory using the library function *malloc*. For entry-level C programming, we recommend sticking to array notation. It's bulkier but much less error prone.

Strings

Strings are any quoted series of characters such as:

```
"Hello, World!"
```

Character strings are a special case of array. Specifically, a string is an array of characters terminated with a null character, which is notated *\0*.

The string in Table 4.7, *my_string*, is an array with 14 elements. The 14th element, which we access using *my_string[13]*, is the null character. It's an important part of the string we must not forget, even though we never see it!

Table 4.7 Character String as an Array

String my_string													
0	1	2	3	4	5	6	7	8	9	10	11	12	13
H	e	l	l	o	,	*space*	W	o	r	l	d	!	\0

As with any other array, a character string can be declared either with a pointer or with array notation.

```
/* declares a pointer to unallocated space of a string of unknown length */
char *pointer_to_string;

/*creates an array for a string of 10 characters and allocates the space */
char array_of_string[10];
```

The correct amount of space is allocated if you assign a value to the string at the same time that you declare it:

```
char *pointer_to_string = "Hello, World!";
char array_of_string[] = "Hello, World!";
```

Both of these declarations allocate enough space for 14 character strings and populate the strings with the assigned value. As with any other array, we strongly recommend using array notation rather than pointer notation to deal with strings. It is very bulky to guess ahead of time how many characters you would like to allocate, and when you become more comfortable with pointer notation you will probably switch to that style because it is more space efficient. But for now, you will find your code much easier to debug if you stick with array notation.

NEED TO KNOW… WARNING ABOUT UNALLOCATED MEMORY

C will not stop you from accessing data you have not allocated. For example, if you allocate an array large enough to hold five integers,

```
int my_array[5];
```

There is nothing in the language preventing you from later trying to grab the 23rd element of the array.

```
int my_number;
my_number = my_array[23];
```

But since you haven't reserved that memory for the array, you have no control over what information might be present in it. It might be empty, or it might be filled with garbage. Or, if that memory doesn't belong to your program, it might crash.

Attempting to read or write unallocated memory might well be the number-one cause of debugging frustration and cursing at computers for a beginner C programmer. A program that looks perfectly valid will suddenly crash, presenting a message similar to:

```
Segmentation violation, core dumped.
```

This happens so frequently that way back in 1980, Greg Boyd at Digital Equipment Corporation wrote a song about it: "The segmentation violation core dumped blues" (see the lyrics at www.netspace.org/~dmacks/internet-songbook/core-dump-blues.html). Nearly 25 years later, it still happens. Just make sure that you allocate unassigned memory before you read it!

Structures

After all the complexity of arrays and pointers, structures are mercifully simple. A structure, or *struct*, contains some number of other data types, all conveniently grouped together. In fact, a *struct* can contain other *structs*:

```
/* struct to hold some important info about a tv show */
struct tv_show {
        int channel;
        char show_name[50];
        char favorite_actor[50];
};

struct show_to_record {
        struct tv_show show_I_like;
        long time;
};
```

Now we can declare and assign a variable of type *show_to_record*:

```
struct show_to_record IronChef;
struct show_to_record Friends;

IronChef.time = 4;
```

```
IronChef.show_I_like.channel = 102;
IronChef.show_I_like.show_name = "Iron Chef";
IronChef.show_I_like.favorite_actor = "Fukui-San";
```

See how you access the elements of the *struct*? If you call the *struct* by its declared name and follow with a dot (.) and the name of the member, you can assign a value to that member. When a *struct* contains a *struct*, you can add another dot, followed by the name of that *struct's* member, and so on. You have to allocate space for all members of a *struct*. If you're using pointers or arrays of unspecified size, you'll need to explicitly allocate the space for them.

Function Calls and Variable Passing

A *function* is a piece of code that is separately defined and can be run as many times as you like. It is essentially a subroutine. The C function *printf* we've been using is an example of a system library-provided function.

Once you've written a function, you need some way to pass your variable to it. There are two ways of dealing with variable data in C: *call by reference* and *call by value*. A variable that has been called by value has a *copy* of its data passed to the function, not the data itself. If you make changes to the variable in the function, you have *not* made those changes to the variable in the main program.

So how do we use a function to make changes that persist in the main program? The first method is simple if you are only changing one variable. A function returns a value (just like any other variable, it can return a value of standard data type such as *int, char,* or the like). If you're only modifying, say, one string, you can have a function that returns a value of type *string* (that is, a pointer to character, or *char* *), as shown in Figure 4.16.

Figure 4.16 A Sample Function Declaration

```
/*
 * this function returns a value of type pointer to char,
 * or "char *"
 */
char *my_function();
```

This solution isn't without drawbacks. For one thing, you might want to modify several variables in one function. For another thing, there is a convention that many functions follow which return integers containing their success status (0 if the function succeeded or 1 if there was an error). If you want that functionality, you can't return both a status integer and a modified variable, but only one.

There's an interesting little side effect to C's use of pointers that gives an excellent workaround. Let's say the function in Figure 4.16 is passed a character string:

```
char *my_function(char *);
```

This format means that *my_function* is a function that takes one variable, a pointer to *char* (presumably a character string), and that returns one variable, also a pointer to *char*. Let's call this function:

```
/* since "char *" is another way of referring to "char[]", */
/* either syntax can be used for declaration */
char some_string[] = "here is my string";

/* now pass it to the function */
my_function(*some_string);
```

We've learned the C uses call by value passing in function calls. So what is being passed to *my_function* here? Is it a copy of the entire character array passed—"here is my string"? No, in fact it's a copy of the *pointer* that points to the character string *some_string*. It's not the same pointer, but they both point to exactly the same place. So if you modify *some_string*, you actually are modifying the string itself. This is how C approximates *call by reference*. The function is being passed a value but that value is a copy of a reference. In this way, you can modify any information that lives outside a function from inside a function. All you need to do is pass a pointer to the variable.

System Calls and Hardware Access

Sometimes your program needs to interact directly with the operating system or hardware. For this we have *system calls*. These will be different on every operating system you use, because they depend on the abilities of the individual operating system and hardware platform. You will probably need to include a system call-specific library file at the beginning of your program; check the documentation for your particular operating system and hardware platform.

System calls are usually necessary for the kinds of low-level hardware access you need if you're writing a device driver. For example, you probably have access to the calls *read* and *write*, which read and write bytes directly from some file descriptor. To properly use these functions, you need some information about the hardware. For example, you probably need to know the physical device's *block size*—a bit of information about the physical device's logical storage mechanism.

You may also have access to some basic file systems calls: *open*, *creat* (yes, that's spelled *creat*, with no *e* on the end), *close*, and *unlink*. These allow you to manipulate files at a level very close to the operating system, instead of in the higher-level functions that are part of the standard library *<stdio.h>*.

You'll need to know a little bit about the structure of your file system and the devices you mean to access if you'll be using system calls. Since system calls are the only way to get close access to the hardware in C, you'll almost certainly need them if you'll be writing any programs that access hardware components directly, such as a device driver to control a sound card.

Summary

C is a powerful language, and we have only introduced a small amount of what it can do. Most of what we've introduced here we've only touched on lightly, and there are many C features we haven't had time to discuss, including such important topics as:

- Enums
- Pointer arithmetic
- Bitwise operators (<<, >>, &, ^, |)
- Logical operators (&&, | |, !)
- Order of precedence
- The standard libraries (primarily string and file functions)
- Variable scope
- Void types
- Explicit type casting

If you plan to write a lot of C, we strongly recommend the books in the "Additional Reading" section of this chapter.

Debugging

Chances are, it won't take you long after you've written your first program to discover your first bug. Everybody, from curious hackers to professionals with decades of experience, makes programming errors. Although it might be easy to find the bug in a five-line program, it can be a lot harder as your programs get more complex. So how do you track down your bugs?

Debugging Tools

Many integrated development environments come with built-in graphical debuggers. These tools allow you to track exactly what your program is doing at any given point in time. Do you think your program is having problems entering your function *make_everything_work()*? Then drag the *stop here* icon, which might look like a little stop sign or an exclamation mark (check your program's documentation), to the line of the program right before it enters that function. When you run the program in your graphical debugger, it will run to that point and then stop and wait for you. You can tell the debugger to step through one line at a time, reporting the contents of variables to you as it goes. This can be a very easy way to discover the reason why your program is crashing.

If you don't have a built-in debugger, or if you prefer the command line, there are tools that you can use. The GNU debugger, or gdb (www.gnu.org/directory/gdb.html), is open source and freely available on a very large number of hardware and software platforms. The GNU project also supplies a graphical front-end to gdb and other command-line debuggers, called DDD (www.gnu.org/software/ddd). Some programmers find command-line tools far more powerful, because they can quickly type any command they need rather than looking in a menu; others find it frustrating not to have the visual aid of a graphical tool while doing complex debugging.

The *printf* Method

Sometimes you have a very short program, and you're pretty sure you know where the bug is. Starting up a debugging program is cumbersome for you, and you don't really want to bother or you might not have a debugger available—all you need to know is the value of a variable before, during, and after you enter your function. This is where homemade debugging comes in.

Just tell your program to print the values of the questionable variable at various points during your program's run. This doesn't work particularly well if you're programming graphics, but for straight text output, it's reasonably effective.

For example:

```
int foo;


printf("before I enter the function, foo is %d\n", foo");
/* Enter the function my_function_works */
my_function_works();
printf("after the function, foo is %d\n", foo");


int my_function_works ()
{
        printf("when I am in the function, foo is %d\n", foo");
        ...
        /* Do some stuff here */
}
```

Need to Know… An Interesting Note About *printf* and Unallocated Memory

If the reason your program is crashing is that you are accessing data from an unallocated pointer, trying to print the data pointed to can crash your program, too! After all, if the data doesn't exist, it's invisible to the *printf* you're using for debugging.

What if you want to leave your debugging information in the program, but for now, you just want it to run without output? Here's a quick and dirty way to turn your debugging on and off. It relies on the C preprocessor *#define* command. We'll also use two new commands*: #ifdef* and *#endif.* These are preprocessor commands (which is the reason for the different syntax; don't worry for now about the distinction between normal commands and preprocessor commands) and they act as simple tests. If the string after an *#ifdef* statement has been defined with a *#define* statement, all lines of code between the *#ifdef* and the *#endif* will be included in the program. If the string has not been defined with a *#define* statement, those lines of code will not be complied nor included in the program. This is a little confusing, so an example could prove helpful:

```
#define DEBUG    /* when this line exists, print out debugging information */


int foo;


#ifdef DEBUG
        /* Only print this error if we are in debug mode */
        printf("before I enter the function, foo is %d\n", foo");
#endif


/* Enter the function my_function_works */
my_function_works();


#ifdef DEBUG
        /* Only print this error if we are in debug mode */
        printf("after the function, foo is %d\n", foo");
#endif

int my_function_works ()
{
#ifdef DEBUG
        /* Only print this error if we are in debug mode */
        printf("when I am in the function, foo is %d\n", foo");
#endif
       ...
       /* Do some stuff here */
}
```

Those lines that are between the *#ifdef* and *#endif* statements won't be evaluated unless *DEBUG* is defined at the beginning of the program. When you want debugging lines in your program, define *DEBUG.* When you want to program to work without debugging, just remove that *#define* statement.

NEED TO KNOW... A NOTE ABOUT PREPROCESSOR COMMANDS

Lines that begin with a # in C are preprocessor commands, which means that they are parsed by the compiler before anything else. Because these lines are processed before any other parts of the code, they are evaluated in order, from top to bottom. The preprocessor ignores function declarations and other control structures that affect the order in which your code is run.

One last note for the sake of completeness: Operating systems generally have concepts of *output streams*, primarily *standard error* (*stderr*) and *standard output* (*stdout*). The theory is that all normal output should go to the standard output stream, and all errors should go to the standard error stream. Usually both standard output and standard error end up on your computer monitor, and when you see the text appear, you don't know—nor do you care—which stream you're seeing. But if you use the appropriate output stream, it's very easy to treat the streams differently. Perhaps you want to pipe all the output of the program into a text file for later analysis, but you want error messages to appear on your screen, not in the text file. Perhaps you don't want to see errors at all. To accommodate this kind of after-the-fact output manipulation, you can use a modified version of the *printf* function to send your errors directly to standard error:

```
fprintf(stderr, "when I am in the function, foo is %d\n", foo");
```

All this debugging will be much simpler if you have used meaningful variable names and commented your code extensively. Debugging a program that crashes for no apparent reason is much more annoying than writing a few extra lines of comments.

Introduction to Assembly Language

Sometimes, even a relatively low-level language such as C doesn't get us close enough to the hardware. A C program can be portable between different platforms and as such it loses something in efficiency. In assembly language, though, every machine instruction possible on that hardware has an assembly language translation. We use assembly language rather than writing directly in machine language, because it is easier to say *ADD address_1 address_2* than to say *0xbe 0x1234 0xf337*. Some would say that a pure assembly language has no instructions that don't map directly to a machine instruction, but we shall stay out of that philosophical battle.

Because of this strong correlation between a particular piece of hardware's instruction set and the assembly language usable on that hardware, assembly language programs aren't particularly portable. A program you write on one system might not be in the slightest bit usable on another system. On the other hand, assembly language programs run extremely quickly and efficiently. Instead of trusting a compiler to lay out the instructions in the most efficient manner, you can guarantee efficiency by writing the instructions exactly as they will be run by the CPU. Moreover, your hardware may have special features that are not accessible to you from a higher-level language such as C.

NEED TO KNOW… LIMITATIONS OF THIS CHAPTER

As you can probably guess from the previous paragraphs, which assembler you use will vary based on your operating system and hardware platform. But even on any given platform, there are many different assembly language implementations you can use. On Intel, for example, you can use such assembly languages as A386, GNU *as*, HLA, SpAsm, and MASM. Some of these are relatively high-level, offering features that we think of as belonging to high-level programming languages, such as *if/else* statements and *while* loops. Others are very simple, offering not much above the level of the hardware. For this chapter, we focus on simple features and give examples using the low-level GNU assembler, *as*, for the Intel 80386 processor.

Components of an Assembly Language Statement

An assembly language statement has four components:

- The label
- The operation
- The operands
- The comments

We examine all these concepts in detail in the subsequent sections.

Labels

Have you ever done any BASIC programming with *GOTOs*? If you have, did somebody give you a supercilious sneer and say, "*Real* programmers don't use *GOTOs*"? Well, now you can sneer right back—because anybody who can program in assembly language *is* a real programmer, and in assembly language, you use *GOTOs*. Oh, we call them *labels*, but don't let that fool you.

If you haven't used labels or *GOTO* statements before, don't worry. The concept is very simple. A label records the memory address of the line of code that contains the label. At any point in the code, your program can *jump* to the memory address of the label:

```
/*
 * Some assembly language code goes here.
 *
 * Do you recognize these lines?  They're comments. In GNU as,
 * any text between "/*" and the next "*/" is a comment,
 * even if it appears in the middle of a line. The comment character
 * may differ (sometimes it is a semicolon (;) or a pound sign (#),
 * for example), but the general format is the same.  These lines
 * will not be translated into machine language.
 */
```

```
my_label:             /* The label is the word and colon at line's start */
    movl $1, %eax     /* Don't worry about what this assembly language */
                      /* command means for now. */

/* More assembly language code goes here. */

jmp my_label          /* now the program will loop back to that label, so */
                      /* the next line of code it executes will be */
                      /* "movl $1, %eax" */
```

If all you do is loop under any condition back to the label, this program will just make endless circles back and forth between *my_label* and the command *jmp my_label*. But even low-level assembly languages provide simple conditionals. In GNU *as*, you can base the decision whether or not to make the jump based on the result of a comparison (Table 4.8).

Table 4.8 GNU *as* Jump Commands

GNU as Command	Function
cmpl value_1 value_2	This as statement compares two values and stores a comparison based on the result. It can be followed by one of the *jump* commands, which will make a decision based on the results of the comparison.
je label	Jump to label if *value_1* equals *value_2*.
jg label	Jump to label if *value_2* is greater than *value_1*.
jge label	Jump to label if *value_2* is greater than or equal to *value_1*.
jl label	Jump to label if *value_2* is less than *value_1*.
jle label	Jump to label if *value_2* is less than or equal to *value_1*.
jmp label	Jump to label no matter what. This statement does not need to be preceded by the comparison.

Operations

Two sorts of operations are possible in assembly language. The first maps directly to machine language instructions (*opcodes*) and is translated directly into machine language by the assembler. The second is a meta-command, a command that tells the assembler to do something, instead of telling the computer to do something. In GNU *as*, a meta-command is always preceded by a dot (.) character. This is good shorthand to remember. Even though we haven't introduced either command to you, you know that *.int* is a command directly to the assembler and *popl* translates to a machine instruction. (Just so you know, *.int* reserves storage for some number of integers, and *popl* pops off the top value of the stack.)

Operands

First, a bit of terminology: An *operand* is the object of an operation. In the following equation the numbers 3 and 5 are both operands (and the + is the *operator*):

```
3 + 5 = ?
```

The C variables often act as special cases of operands. In the C statement, the number 4.0 and the variable *my_number* are both operands:

```
my_answer = my_number / 4.0;
```

When you read about operands with assembly languages, for all practical purposes you're reading about variable assignment.

We learned in the C section of this chapter that different kinds of data take up different amounts of space. In GNU *as*, we declare the data by type in order to guarantee enough space.

The possible data types are:

- **byte** For a single byte of computer memory.
- **int** For an integer between 0 and 65,535.
- **long** For an integer between 0 and 4,294,967,295.
- **ascii** For one or more characters.

The data storage is declared in the special section of the assembly language program, which is initiated with a statement to the assembler:

```
.section .data
```

Next then the storage itself is declared, with another command to the assembler:

```
.ascii "Hello, world\0"
```

In C, character strings were automatically terminated with the null character (\0). In assembly language, you'll need to add that terminating character by hand.

Sample Program

The best way to understand assembly language is to see a little bit of it. Here's a simple program that does a little bit of addition:

```
 /* addition.exe */
 /*
 * sample assembly language program in GNU as
 * adds together the numbers "3" and "17"
 */

 /* Data section.  We're not using any variables here - just holding
 * the arguments from the command line in registers, so this
 * section is blank. */

.section .data

/* Text section.  This section contains the actual program. */

.section .text

/* .globl defines a label which has to exist even from outside the program.
 * "_start" is a special-purpose label which tells the program that this is
 * the beginning, similar to "main()" in C. */

.globl _start
_start:

pushl $17             /* push the number 17 onto the top of the stack */
                      /* the stack is the part of memory which is currently */
                      /* being used. Think of it like a stack of cafeteria trays.*/
pushl $3              /* push the number 3 onto the top of the stack. */
                      /* now 3 is on top, with 17 beneath it. */
```

```
popl %eax           /* pop the top of value on the stack (3) -- that is, */
                    /* remove it from the stack, and put it in the */
                    /* temporary register "%eax" */

popl %ebx           /* pop the top of value on the stack (17) -- that is, */
                    /* remove it from the stack, and put it in the */
                    /* temporary register "%ebx" */

addl %eax, %ebx     /* add together the two numbers, and store the result */
                    /* in the second temporary register, %ebx */

movl $1, %eax       /* in Linux, this is the kernel's system call */
                    /* to exit the program.  When the program exits, */
                    /* whatever value is stored in register %ebx */
                    /* will be the return value of the program. */
                    /* because of our addl command, the value stored */
                    /* in %ebx is the sum of 3+17 */

int $0x80           /* this runs the software interrupt responsible */
                    /* for telling the kernel to exit */
```

After we run this program, we can test the return value of the program to find out the sum of the two numbers. As you might guess from looking at the program, we made this somewhat more complex than it needed to be. We didn't need to push 3 and 17 onto the stack, then pop them both off again in order to add them together. We could have just stored the two numbers directly into the temporary registers. But the purpose of the example was to give you a taste of assembly language.

Need to Know… Stack Trickiness

The top of the stack is in reality the bottom of the stack. Yes, we know, that makes no sense. After all, both "top" and "bottom" are just fake names—what do they really mean in a computer's memory? It's not like there is gravity in the computer defining what is "top" and what is "bottom." What these terms mean is that if you think of memory addresses as having higher numbers at the top and lower numbers at the bottom, the stack grows downward, as illustrated in Table 4.9.

Table 4.9 Stack Direction

Memory That Holds the Stack	Stack Sitting in Memory
Address 22	First entry placed into stack
Address 18	Second entry placed into stack
Address 16	Third entry placed into stack
Address 12	Current top of stack
Address 8	X
Address 4	X
Address 0	X

If we now choose to place another entry in the stack, it will go to address 8. So if we need to manually manipulate the *stack pointer* (stored in register *%esp*), adding a new entry to the stack means *subtracting* from the value of the stack pointer.

Summary

The basis of assembly language is simple to learn. However, learning how to do something with it—that is a whole new kettle of fish.

In general, assembly language is only used to manipulate hardware we can't access with high-level languages or to accelerate a particularly slow section of code. However some coders prefer using assembly over a high-level language, and it is particularly useful for hardware hacking.

Additional Reading

If you are interested in learning more about any of the topics in this chapter, we recommend the following books:

- ***Structured Computer Organization,*** **fourth edition, by Andrew S. Tannenbaum (Prentice-Hall, 1998)**
- ***A Book on C,*** **by Al Kelley and Ira Pohl (The Benjamin/Cummings Publishing Company, 1995)**
- ***C Programming Language,*** **second edition, by Brian W. Kernighan and Dennis Ritchie (Prentice Hall, 1988)**
- ***The Art of Assembly Language,*** **by Randall Hyde (No Starch Press, 2003 or http://webster.cs.ucr.edu)**
- ***Programming from the Ground Up,*** **by Jonathan Bartlett (http://savannah.nongnu.org/projects/pgubook)**